THIRD EDITION

STORIES
WE BROUGHT
WITH US

BEGINNING READINGS

Carol Kasser • Ann Silverman

Longman

We dedicate this book to our parents.

C.K. and A.S.

Stories We Brought with Us

Copyright © 2002 by Pearson Education, Inc.
All rights reserved.
No part of this publication may be reproduced,
stored in a retrieval system or transmitted
in any form or by any means, electronic, mechanical,
photocopying, recording, or otherwise,
without the prior permission of the publisher.

Pearson Education, 10 Bank Street, White Plains, NY 10606

Vice president, director of publishing: Allen Ascher
Editorial director: Louisa Hellegers
Acquisitions editor: Laura Le Dréan
Senior development manager: Penny Laporte
Development editor: Andrea Bryant
Vice president, director of design and production: Rhea Banker
Director of electronic production: Aliza Greenblatt
Executive managing editor: Linda Moser
Senior production editor: Christine Lauricella
Production supervisor: Ray Keating
Associate art director: Pat Wosczyk
Director of manufacturing: Patrice Fraccio
Senior manufacturing buyer: Dave Dickey
Cover and text design: Pat Wosczyk
Text composition: Monika Popowitz
Text art and cover: Penny Carter

Library of Congress Cataloging-in-Publication Data

Stories we brought with us: beginning readings/[compiled by] Carol Kasser, Ann Silverman.
    p. cm.
  ISBN 0-13-028462-9 (alk. paper)
    1. English language--Textbooks for foreign speakers. 2. Readers. 3. Tales I. Kasser,
Carol. II. Silverman, Ann.

    PE1128.S863 2001
    428.6'4--dc21   2001038016

2 3 4 5 6 7 8 9 10—VHG—06 05 04 03 02

Contents

The idea for *Stories We Brought with Us* came from our students' interest in reading and telling stories that were handed down to them by their parents, grandparents, and teachers in their own countries. Some of the stories in this book may already be familiar to your students; others may not be. We hope that students will react to the stories, ask questions, make comments, tell other versions, and relate stories from their own countries.

Each story is presented twice. Version A uses less complex structures and more limited vocabulary. Version B uses a greater variety of sentence structures and is more idiomatic. Telling the story twice allows both teachers and students a great deal of flexibility, since many ESL classes include students at different reading levels. For example, in some classes, one group of students might read version A, while another group reads version B. In other classes, all students might read both versions, which allows them to grasp the story line and characters in version A so that when they read version B, they can be more attentive to structure and vocabulary. Accordingly, each story has two sets of exercises. Not all students will necessarily do all the exercises. Choice of exercises will depend on how your own class uses the book. In all cases, students should do the Before You Read exercise at the beginning of each chapter, and the Discussion and Writing exercises at the end of each chapter.

Every chapter begins with one or more illustrations. Some show a variety of scenes in the story, and others depict the main idea. These illustrations, along with the Before You Read questions, are an excellent springboard for discussion.

Beneath each story title the country or region of origin is given. In many cases, more than one country has claimed a story. We did our best to find out to which country each story is most often attributed, but in some cases we were unable to identify the origin of these tales. Those stories are listed as "traditional folktales." Where we do list origins, you may find that some students disagree. If this happens, encourage the students to discuss what they know about the folktale.

Following the opening page you will find Comprehension, Vocabulary, and Grammar exercises for both versions of the stories. Where appropriate, we have included Dictionary Skills exercises and Spelling and Pronunciation exercises. Each chapter concludes with Discussion and Writing and Just for Fun. At the end of the book is a glossary of words that some students may find challenging.

In addition, you may want to try these activities with your classes:

1. **Dictation:** After students have read and are familiar with the story, dictate a paragraph one sentence at a time, at normal speed. You can also do a cloze dictation using photocopies of a paragraph, or dictate the whole story with every nth word left blank.

2. **Read and Look Up:** To encourage students to read at the sentence level rather than word by word, ask them to read a sentence or short paragraph and then look up. Then, ask for the information from that sentence or paragraph.

3. **Rewrite:** Ask the students to rewrite the story, either individually or in groups.

4. **Retell:** Ask the students to retell the story in their own words. They may want to use the illustrations in the book as a guide. (For example, the illustrations for "The Ant and the Cicada" form a sequence that tells the complete story.) If students have difficulty remembering details and sequence, try retelling the story first.

Learning to read in a second language is often hard work, but we think that it can be a source of pleasure and satisfaction for all students. Sharing stories and folktales is one way to encourage such enjoyment. We hope that you and your students will find these stories a rich source of learning – both about each other and the English language.

ACKNOWLEDGMENTS

This book has benefited from the help of many people. In particular, we would like to express our gratitude to our professors, Virginia French Allen and Donald Knapp, who inspired a generation of teachers by their example.

We gratefully acknowledge the suggestions of our colleagues at the Community College of Philadelphia, the enthusiasm and support of Beth and Pierre Montagano, and the patience and skill of our editors—Laura Le Dréan, Acquisitions Editor, Andrea Bryant, Development Editor, and Chris Lauricella, Senior Production Editor—in helping to make this edition of *Stories We Brought with Us* a reality.

Most of all, we thank our students, who brought these stories with them.

Chapter 1

A LESSON IN PERSISTENCE

a traditional folktale

BEFORE YOU READ A and B

1. Look at the picture. Do you think the story will be about a young person or an old person? A man or a woman? Does the story take place in the city or the country? Explain why you think so.

2. When people have *persistence*, they continue to do something for a long time, even when other people think it is wrong or foolish. Can you think of something you persist in doing because you know it is right? Can you think of something you or others persist in doing even though it is wrong?

3. Is persistence always good? What do you think about each of the following?

    - an athlete who persists in practicing
    - a child who persistently asks for candy
    - a person with a persistent cough
    - a dog that barks persistently
    - a person who tries persistently to find a job

WHILE YOU READ

1. The title says this story will teach you a lesson. As you read the story, try to guess what the lesson is.

2. As you read, decide whether the old man's persistence is good or bad. Be prepared to explain your answer.

■ ■ ■

A LESSON IN PERSISTENCE

1   A long time ago, there was an old man who was very patient. Every day, he sat in front of his house doing the same job. He was patiently sharpening a piece of iron.

2   One day, his neighbor saw him at work. He asked the man, "What are you doing?" The old man said, "I want to make this iron into a needle."

3   The neighbor was surprised because the piece of iron was big, and a needle is very small. He asked the man, "How long will it take you to finish making the needle?"

4   The old man answered, "I don't know. If I die before I finish, I will leave this work for my son. And if my son dies before it is finished, he will leave this work for my grandchildren. Someday, this piece of iron will be a needle."

COMPREHENSION

1 *Write* **T** *next to the sentences that are* **true**. *Write* **F** *next to the sentences that are* **false**. *The first one is done for you.*

1. __T__ The man worked at home.

2. ____ The old man worked quickly.

3. ____ The old man was patient.

4. ____ The old man might not finish the job himself.

5. ____ The old man was persistent.

2 *Circle the letter of the word or words that best completes each sentence. The first one is done for you.*

1. This story happened _____ .
   a. today
   b. yesterday
   c. a long time ago *(circled)*

2. The man in the story was _____ .
   a. young
   b. old
   c. middle-aged

3. The man wanted to make _____ .
   a. a piece of iron
   b. a needle
   c. a house

4. The neighbor was _____ .
   a. surprised
   b. happy
   c. persistent

5. Making the needle will probably take _____ .
   a. one day
   b. a few weeks
   c. many years

VOCABULARY

1 *Complete the sentences with words from the list. The first one is done for you.*

finished	iron	patiently	sharpening
needle	neighbor	grandchildren	
persistence	piece	surprised	

1. The man worked _patiently_ at his job.

2. Jim was _____ his knife so that it would cut better.

3. Amy was using a _____ and thread to sew a dress.

4. It is important to have _____ when you do a difficult job.

5. My _____ lives across the street.

6. Virginia was very _____ when she saw her present.

7. Have you _____ your homework yet?

8. Would you like a _____ of candy?

9. The worker used _____ to make steel.

10. The children of my children are my _____ .

2 *Look back at the story. Find the sentence in the paragraph shown in parentheses. Then, find the words that mean the same as the underlined words. The first one is done for you.*

1. <u>Daily</u>, he sat in front of his house doing the same <u>task</u>. (paragraph 1)

   daily *every day*

   task ___*job*___

2. The old man <u>responded</u>, "I don't know." (paragraph 4).

   responded _____

3. "And if my son dies before it is <u>completed</u>, he will leave this work for my grandchildren." (paragraph 4)

   completed _____

GRAMMAR

1 *Complete the sentences with the correct form of each word. The first one is done for you.*

patience	patient	patiently

1. It is important to have _**patience**_ with children.

2. You must be very _____ when you study a new language.

3. Joe worked slowly and _____ on the assignment.

persist	persistent	persistently	persistence

4. If you study _____, you will learn English.

5. Sometimes it is hard to _____ in your studies when you are busy.

6. But with a little _____ you can learn English and do well in school.

7. If you are _____, all of your hard work will pay off.

surprise	surprised	surprising	surprisingly

8. The cat _____ me when it jumped on me.

9. There is a _____ for you on the desk.

10. Betty and Jill did _____ well in the race.

11. It is _____ how well you can do if you persist.

2 Notice how the verb **take** is used in the question **How long will it take you to finish?** Practice asking questions with **how long** and **take**. Ask a partner the following questions and report the answers to the class.

1. How long does it take you to go home from school every day?

2. How long did it take you to eat your dinner last night?

3. How long does it take you to get dressed in the morning?

4. How long will it take you to complete your courses?

PRONUNCIATION AND SPELLING

1 Ten of the following words contain the /**sh**/ sound. Say each word aloud or repeat after your teacher, and circle the words with the /**sh**/ sound. The first one is done for you.

(finished)	grandchildren	lesson	machine	national
ocean	patiently	surely	racial	sharpening
special	permission	surprised	teacher	which

2 **Homophones** are words that sound the same but have different spellings, such as **here** and **hear**. English has many homophones including:

I / eye	no / know	piece / peace
so / sew	too / two	would / wood

Complete the sentences with words from the list. Use a dictionary if you need help. The first one is done for you.

1. The doctor told me to close my right _____ eye _____ .

2. A bicycle has _____ wheels.

3. Where _____ you like to go?

4. People use needles when they _____ .

5. The old man had a _____ of iron.

6. We don't _____ the man's name.

7. We get _____ from trees.

8. Tell me yes or _____.

9. Patricia was tired, _____ she sat down.

10. Candy is sweet, and cake is, _____.

11. Why is there war when everyone wants _____?

12. My sister and _____ went to the movies yesterday.

WHILE YOU READ

1. The title says this story will teach you a lesson. As you read the story, try to guess what the lesson is.

2. As you read, decide whether the old man's persistence is good or bad. Be prepared to explain your answer.

A LESSON IN PERSISTENCE

1   Long ago, there lived an old man who sat patiently working in his front yard every day. He was slowly sharpening a piece of iron. His only tool was a file.

2   One day, his neighbor saw him at work and asked him what he was doing. The old man explained that he wanted to make the iron into a needle.

3   The neighbor was very surprised to hear that, because the piece of iron was very big, and a needle is very, very tiny. He asked, "Won't it take many years to finish making the needle?"

4   The old man responded that he did not know how long it would take to finish the job of making the needle. But if he died before it was completed, he would leave the work for his son. And if his son died before it was finished, he would leave it for the old man's grandchildren. Someday, the piece of iron would become a needle.

COMPREHENSION

Answer the following questions in pairs or small groups.

1. What was the old man making?

2. How long will it take for the old man to finish?

3. Why was the neighbor surprised?

4. What will happen to the piece of iron if the old man can't finish his work?

5. Why is this story called "A Lesson in Persistence"?

VOCABULARY

1 *Match the words in the first column with their definitions in the second column. The first one is done for you.*

1. _g_ a yard
2. _____ sharpening
3. _____ a tool
4. _____ a file
5. _____ explained
6. _____ tiny
7. _____ responded
8. _____ completed

a. an instrument used to make things smooth
b. very small
c. an instrument used to make or repair things
d. answered
e. making a point or an edge
f. gave reasons for; made clear
g. the land around a house or building
h. finished

2 *Three words in each of these rows have almost the same meaning. One word has a different meaning. Circle the word that has a different meaning. Use your dictionary if you need help. The first one is done for you.*

1. make   produce   (take)   create
2. answer   finish   reply   respond
3. surprised   amazed   afraid   astonished
4. old   happy   ancient   elderly
5. working   laboring   toiling   asking

3 *Circle the correct answers. The first one is done for you.*

1. Which of the following are tools?
   (files)   (hammers)   yards
   neighbors   (saws)   tables

2. Which of the following are metals?
   copper   cotton   gold   meat
   iron   silver   tin   wood

3. Which of the following are people?
   babies   cars   daughters   grandchildren
   needles   sons   neighbors   houses

4 *Look back at the story. Find the sentence in the paragraph shown in parentheses. Then, find the words that mean the same as the underlined words.*

1. The neighbor was very <u>amazed</u> to hear that because the piece of iron was very <u>huge,</u> and a needle is very, very tiny. (paragraph 3)

   amazed _____

   huge _____

2. The old man <u>replied</u> that he <u>was unsure</u> how long it would take to <u>complete</u> the <u>task</u> of making the needle. (paragraph 4)

   replied _____

   was unsure _____

   complete _____

   task _____

DICTIONARY SKILLS

Dictionaries often have more than one definition of a word. Look at the three words below and their definitions. Then, write the letter of the definition of the word as used in each sentence. The first one is done for you.

iron

   a. (*noun*) a common heavy metal

   b. (*noun*) an instrument with a flat bottom that is heated and used to smooth clothes

   c. (*verb*) to smooth clothes with a heated instrument with a flat bottom

1. The man was sharpening a piece of <u>iron</u>.   <u>a</u>

2. I have to <u>iron</u> my dress so it will look nice.   _____

patient

   a. (*noun*) a person who is getting medical treatment

   b. (*adjective*) able to wait calmly for a long time

3. The old man was very <u>patient</u>.   _____

4. The doctor gave his <u>patient</u> some medicine.   _____

needle

    a. (*noun*) a small, thin, pointed piece of steel or metal used for sewing

    b. (*noun*) a small, thin, pointed instrument used by doctors to put medicine into a person

5. The woman was looking for a <u>needle</u> and thread so she could sew a button on her coat. _____

6. The baby cried when the doctor gave him a <u>needle</u> in his arm. _____

GRAMMAR

There are two ways to report what someone says. *Direct speech* reports exactly what someone said and uses quotation marks. *Indirect speech* reports the idea of what someone said and does not use quotation marks. Look at the following examples:

    Direct: The man's neighbors said, "We are surprised."

    Indirect: The man's neighbors said that they were surprised.

What differences do you see between direct speech and indirect speech? Look at the punctuation, the verb tenses, and the pronouns.

Read each of the following sentences in indirect speech. Then complete the sentences below in direct speech. The first one is done for you.

1. The old man answered that he wanted to make a needle.

    The old man answered, _____ **"I want to make a needle."** _____

2. Then he said that he didn't know how long it would take.

    Then he said, _____

3. He also told his neighbor that he would leave the work for his son.

    He also told his neighbor, _____

2 *Combine each pair of sentences to make one sentence with the same meaning. Use the word in parentheses to connect the two sentences. The first one is done for you.*

1. This story is about an old man. He was making a needle.

   (who) <u>This story is about an old man who was making a needle.</u>

2. The man had a piece of iron. It was very large.

   (that) _____

3. Tailors are people. They use needles in their work.

   (who) _____

4. Iron is a metal. It is hard and strong.

   (that) _____

5. Hammers are tools. They are much bigger than needles.

   (that) _____

6. A needle is a long, sharp pin. It has a hole to put thread through.

   (that) _____

PRONUNCIATION AND SPELLING

1 Some words are hard to read aloud because some letters are not pronounced the way they look. For example, words ending in *-tient*, *-tion*, *-tial*, or *-cial* (such as *patient*, *potion*, *partial*, and *social*) have endings that are pronounced **/shunt/**, **/shun/**, and **/shul/**.

Say each word aloud or repeat after your teacher:

   motion   nation   fiction   facial   spatial

*Write two words ending in -**tion** that follow this pronunciation rule.*

   _____tion   _____tion

2 Some words contain letters that are not pronounced at all, such as the *w* in *wrist*, and the *k* in *know*. *W* is not pronounced in the *wr-* combination at the beginning of words, and *k* is not pronounced in the *kn-* combination at the beginning of words.

Say each word aloud or repeat after your teacher:

knot   knife   write   wrong   wrap

Write two more words starting with **kn-** *and two with* **wr-** *where the initial letter is silent.*

kn _____   kn _____   wr _____   wr _____

DISCUSSION AND WRITING A and B

Discuss or write the answers to these questions.

1. A *moral* is a lesson taught by a story. What is the lesson or moral of this story?

2. What did the old man think about persistence? What did the neighbor think about the old man? What do you think? Was he wise or foolish? Why?

3. Tell a story from your country that teaches the importance of persistence.

4. Give an example from your own life or the life of someone you know that shows the importance of persistence.

5. Do you think the piece of iron will ever really become a needle? Why or why not?

6. There is an old saying, "You may not be able to finish the task, but that doesn't excuse you from beginning it." What does that mean? How does it relate to this story?

JUST FOR FUN A and B

Work in pairs to act out the story without words. Use everyday objects, such as pencils, to help you.

Chapter 2

A Wise Wish

a folktale from China

BEFORE YOU READ A and B

1. Look at picture 1. Find the mountains and the river. Some clothes are lying beside the river. Do you think they belong to a cowboy, a king, or a soldier? Why?

2. Look at picture 2. Two people are wearing big hats. What are they doing? Explain why you think so.

3. Have you ever helped someone you didn't like because you knew it was the right thing to do?

WHILE YOU READ

1. Stop after paragraph 1. What do you think will happen next?

2. As you read, think about the actions of the farmers. Would you have done the same thing in their place?

■ ■ ■

A Wise Wish

1   There was once a very bad king. All the people hated him. One hot day the king was walking along the river. He decided to take a swim. The king was a good swimmer, but when he got into the water, he suddenly felt a pain in his side. He started to drown.

2   Two farmers were working in a field nearby. They jumped into the water and saved him. They didn't know that he was the king until he was out of the water.

3   The king was very grateful to the farmers. He said to them, "You have saved my life. Ask me for anything you want." One of the farmers said, "I need two water buffaloes to help me in the fields." The king promised he would give him the animals.

4   Then the king asked the other farmer, "What is your wish?" The other farmer was old and wise. He thought and thought. Then he said, "Don't tell anyone that I helped to save your life."

COMPREHENSION

1 *Write **T** next to the sentences that are **true**. Write **F** next to the sentences that are **false**.*

1. _____ The wise farmer was very glad he saved the king.

2. _____ The farmers didn't know how to swim.

3. _____ The king didn't know how to swim.

4. _____ One farmer asked for two animals.

5. _____ Everyone hated the king.

2 Number the sentences to show the correct story order. The first one is done for you.

_____ The wise man said, "Don't tell anyone."

_____ The two farmers saved the king's life.

__1__ The king was walking along the river.

_____ The king got a pain in his side.

_____ The first farmer asked for water buffaloes.

_____ The king decided to take a swim.

3 Answer the following questions in pairs or small groups.

1. Why did the king decide to take a swim?
2. Why did the king start to drown?
3. Where were the two farmers?
4. What did the first farmer ask for?
5. What did the second farmer ask for?

VOCABULARY

1 Complete the sentences with words from the list.

drown	grateful	jumped	nearby	promised

1. The king was far from home, but there was a farm _____ .

2. The river was deep, and the king went under the water for too long, so he started to _____ .

3. He told the farmers who saved him that he was very _____ .

4. He was glad that they _____ into the water to save him.

5. When he _____ to do something, he always did it.

2 *Circle the correct answers.*

1. Which of the following are people?

   buffaloes   farmers   fields

   kings   rivers   swimmers

2. Which of the following words have the same meaning?

   appreciative   elderly   grateful

   huge   persistent   thankful

3. Which of the following are animals?

   buffaloes   swimmers   farmers

   horses   wishes   cows

GRAMMAR

1 *Complete the sentences with the correct prepositions.*

> for   in   to   with

1. Everybody _____ the town hated him.
2. The king agreed _____ the first farmer's request.
3. The wise old farmer thought _____ a while.
4. He knew the king was unpopular _____ his people.

2 *Complete the sentences with the correct clause connectors.*

> if   that   until   unless   while

1. The king felt hot _____ he was taking a walk.
2. He swam _____ he got a pain in his side.
3. He would have drowned _____ the farmers had not rescued him.
4. He knew he would drown _____ the farmers rescued him.
5. The old man said not to tell anyone _____ he saved the king's life.

WHILE YOU READ

1. Stop after paragraph 1. What do you think will happen next?

2. As you read, think about the actions of the farmers. Would you have done the same thing in their place?

■ ■ ■

A Wise Wish

1   Once there was a very bad king who was unpopular with all his people. One hot day while he was taking a walk by the river, the king decided to go for a swim. He was a good swimmer, but when he got into the water, he got a cramp. He started to drown.

2   Two farmers who were working in a field nearby saw him drowning and jumped in to rescue him. The king thanked them and identified himself. He was so grateful that he gave each farmer one wish.

3   The first farmer asked for a pair of water buffaloes. The king gladly agreed to this request. Then the king asked the second man to state his wish.

4   The second farmer, a wise old man, thought for awhile. Finally he said, "Do not tell anyone that I helped to save your life."

COMPREHENSION

Answer the following questions in pairs or small groups.

1. What happened to the king when he went for a swim?

2. What did the two farmers do when they saw the king drowning?

3. How did the king show his thanks to the farmers?

4. How many water buffaloes did the first farmer want?

5. Why didn't the second farmer want anyone to know that he had saved the king?

VOCABULARY

1 *Match the words in the first column with their definitions in the second column.*

1. _____ unpopular
2. _____ a cramp
3. _____ started
4. _____ a field
5. _____ nearby
6. _____ to rescue
7. _____ a request
8. _____ finally

a. began
b. something asked for
c. not liked
d. after a long time
e. a quick, sharp pain
f. a piece of land for farming
g. to save
h. not far away

2 Sometimes certain letters are added to the beginning of a word to change its meaning. These letters are called a *prefix*. Sometimes letters are added to the end of a word to change the meaning or the grammatical form. These letters are called a *suffix*.

*The prefix **un-** means "not." It changes a word so it means the opposite. Add **un-** to the words below. Then, write a sentence with the new word. The first one is done for you.*

1. popular _____unpopular_____

   That television show was unpopular, so they canceled it.

2. happy _____

   _____

3. wise _____

   _____

*The suffix -**ful** means "full of" or "**having a lot of**." The ending makes a word an adjective. Add –**ful** to the words below. Then, write a sentence with the new word.*

4. help _____

   _____

5. beauty _____ (change the *y* to *i*)

   _____

6. use _____

   _____

*The suffix -**ly** usually makes a word an adverb. Add -**ly** to the words below. Then, write a sentence with the new word.*

7. grateful _____

_____

8. glad _____

_____

9. lazy _____ (change the *y* to *i*)

_____

DICTIONARY SKILLS

*Look at the three definitions of the word **state**. Then, write the letter of the definition of the word as used in each sentence.*

a. (*noun*) the condition of something
b. (*noun*) a country or a smaller part of a country
c. (*verb*) to say in words

1. The king told the man to state his wish. _____

2. The boy was in a very bad state after the accident. _____

3. I live in the state of Pennsylvania. _____

GRAMMAR

*Combine each pair of sentences using **so . . . that** to make one sentence with the same meaning. Notice that **so** replaces **very** in the combined sentence. You will find a sentence using this structure in paragraph 3. The first one is done for you.*

1. The story is very short. We can read it again.

   The story is so short that we can read it again.

2. The king was very bad. All the people hated him.

   _____

3. The king felt very hot. He decided to take a swim.

   _____

4. The king was very grateful. He gave each farmer a wish.

   _____

5. The second farmer was very wise. He thought for a while before he replied.

   _____

PRONUNCIATION AND SPELLING

Four words in each of these rows rhyme, which means that they end with the same sounds. Say each word aloud or repeat after your teacher. Then, circle the one word in each row that does not rhyme. Do not be tricked by the spelling. Pay attention to the <u>sounds</u>*.*

1. to   go   you   do   true
2. brown   down   grown   drown   noun
3. wise   dies   eyes   buys   days
4. bed   bread   paid   said   dead
5. how   know   no   grow   go

DISCUSSION AND WRITING

Discuss or write answers to these questions.

1. The title of the story is "A Wise Wish," but the story tells about two wishes. What were they? Which was the "wise" wish according to the storyteller? Do you agree or disagree? Why?

2. Many countries have stories about people who have a chance to make wishes. Do you know any stories like this? What is the story about?

3. Do you swim? What rules of safety do you follow when you swim?

4. Do you know what rules you should follow if you see someone drowning? Did the farmers do the right thing? What could they have done instead?

5. If you were given one wish, what would you wish for?

6. Pretend that the king is telling the story. Retell or rewrite the story starting with paragraph 2. Remember to change verbs and pronouns when necessary. Start with the sentence, *One day while I was taking a walk by the river, I decided to go for a swim.*

JUST FOR FUN A and B

1. Work in groups of three to act out the story.

2. Write a different last paragraph for the story.

3. What if the story started with these sentences: *There was once a good king. All the people loved him.* How would that change the rest of the story? Working in small groups, write a new story to go with this new beginning.

Chapter 3

The Ant and the Cicada

a traditional folktale

BEFORE YOU READ A and B

1. Look at the pictures. Which are the ants? Which are the cicadas? Describe them.

2. Look at picture 1. What are the ants doing? What are the cicadas doing? Describe the weather.

3. Look at picture 2. What are the ants doing? What are the cicadas doing? Describe the weather.

4. Look at picture 4. Describe the cicadas. What do you think happened to them?

5. Can you think of a time when you didn't prepare for something important?

WHILE YOU READ

1. When you read the story, think about the behavior of the ants and the cicadas. Did the ants do the right thing? Why?

2. Read to the end of paragraph 5. What do you think will happen to the cicadas next?

■ ■ ■

The Ant and the Cicada

1   In the old days, ants and cicadas were friends. They were very different. The ants were hardworking, but the cicadas were lazy.

2   In the summer, the ant families were very busy. They knew that in the winter they would have to stay in their anthill. They wanted to have enough food for the whole winter. While the ants worked hard, the cicadas didn't do anything. They sang and danced all day. When they were hungry, they could fly to the farm and get something to eat.

3   One day, the cicadas were singing and dancing. They saw a long line of ants bringing food to their anthill. The cicadas said, "Stop, my silly friends. It's a very nice day. Come and dance with us." The ants said, "Don't you know about winter? If you don't work now, you'll have trouble later."

4   But the cicadas said, "We have strong wings. We can fly anywhere we want. Stupid ants!" And they continued to sing and dance.

5   In the winter, It rained or snowed all the time and it was very cold. In the anthill, there was singing and dancing. But the cicadas had nothing to eat. They asked the ants for some food. The ants said, "We thought you could fly anywhere. Now who is stupid and silly?"

6   The cicadas cried and said that their wings were wet from the rain. The ants said, "We're sorry, but now it's too late. If we help you, there won't be enough food for us. Sorry, very sorry." And the ants closed their door.

7   The next day, when the ants opened their door, all the cicadas were dead! That's why we can hear cicadas sing in the summer, but in the winter they are silent.

COMPREHENSION

1 *Write* **T** *next to the sentences that are* **true**. *Write* **F** *next to the sentences that are* **false**.

   1. _____ The ants worked hard in the winter.

   2. _____ Cicadas like to sing and dance.

   3. _____ Cicadas can fly.

   4. _____ The cicadas flew south for the winter.

   5. _____ Ants are hardworking.

   6. _____ Ants don't like to sing and dance.

   7. _____ The ants shared their food with the cicadas.

   8. _____ An anthill is an ant's home.

   9. _____ Cicadas don't sing in the winter.

 10. _____ The cicadas were hardworking.

2 *Answer the following questions in pairs or small groups.*

   1. Why did the ants work so hard in the summer?

   2. Who sang and danced in the summer?

   3. Why didn't the cicadas work hard in the summer?

   4. "If you don't work hard now, you'll have trouble later." Who is talking? To whom are they talking? What trouble would come later?

   5. Who sang and danced in the winter?

   6. Why didn't the ants give food to the cicadas?

   7. Why didn't the cicadas fly away in the winter?

   8. What happened to the cicadas in the winter?

VOCABULARY

1 *Complete the sentences with words from the list.*

different	busy	hardworking	silent

1. During a test, students should be _____ .

2. Ron and Bill are twins, but they look _____ from each other.

3. _____ students usually do well in school.

4. The stores are very _____ during the holidays.

2 *Look back at the story. Find the sentence in the paragraph shown in parentheses. Then, find the words that mean the same as the underlined words.*

1. In the winter, it rained and snowed all the time and it was very <u>chilly</u>. (paragraph 5)

    chilly _____

2. The cicadas <u>wept</u> and said their wings were <u>damp</u> from the rain. (paragraph 6)

    wept _____

    damp _____

3. And the ants <u>shut</u> their door. (paragraph 6)

    shut _____

4. That's why we can hear cicadas sing in the summer, but in the winter they are <u>quiet</u>. (paragraph 7)

    quiet _____

GRAMMAR

1 *Look back at the story. Find the sentence in the paragraph shown in parentheses. Then, write who or what the underlined pronouns refer to. The first one is done for you.*

1. <u>They</u> were very different. (paragraph 1)

    they <u>ants and cicadas</u>

2. <u>They</u> wanted to have enough food for the whole winter. (paragraph 2)

    they _____

3. <u>They</u> sang and danced all day. (paragraph 2)

    they _____

4. <u>We</u> have strong wings. (paragraph 4)

we _____

5. <u>We</u> thought <u>you</u> could fly anywhere. (paragraph 5)

we _____ you _____

2 Expressions that describe the weather often begin with *It* and the verb *be*. Sometimes we use an adjective to describe the weather.

Example: It is sunny. It is cold. It is windy.

Other times we use *It* followed by the *present progressive tense*.

Example: It is raining. It is snowing.

Answer these questions about the weather.

1. Look at picture 1 on page 20. Describe the weather in that picture.

_____

2. Look at picture 3 on page 20. Describe the weather in that picture.

_____

3. Describe the weather today.

_____

3 *Combine each pair of sentences using the word* **but** *to make one sentence.* **But** *is used when there is a contrast (difference) between the information in the first half of the sentence and the information in the second half of the sentence. Remember to add a comma. The first one is done for you.*

1. The ants were hardworking. The cicadas were lazy.

<u>The ants were hardworking, but the cicadas were lazy.</u>

2. The ants worked in the summer. The cicadas sang and danced.

_____

3. The ants were happy in the winter. The cicadas were cold and wet.

_____

4. Cicadas can fly. Ants crawl.

_____

5. The ants had food in the winter. The cicadas didn't.

_____

6. Ants and cicadas are insects. Dogs are mammals.

_____

7. The winter was cold. The summer was hot.

_____

B

WHILE YOU READ

1. When you read the story, think about the behavior of the ants and the cicadas. Did the ants do the right thing? Why?

2. Read to the end of paragraph 5. What do you think will happen to the cicadas next?

■ ■ ■

The Ant and the Cicada

1   Long ago, ants and cicadas were friends. The ants were very industrious, but the cicadas were lazy.

2   During the summertime, the ants were busy preparing for winter when they would have to stay in all the time.

3   One day, when the cicadas were singing and dancing, they saw a long line of ants carrying food to their anthill. The cicadas invited the ants to join them. But the ants said, "We have to get ready for the winter. If you don't do the same thing, you'll be sorry later!"

4   The cicadas answered, "We can fly anywhere we want with our strong wings. Stupid ants!" And the cicadas kept on singing and dancing.

5   When the winter came, it was chilly and damp all the time. Inside the anthill, the ants sang and danced. But the cicadas were hungry. They asked the ants if they could borrow some food. The ants said, "We thought you could fly anywhere you wanted!"

6   But the cicadas' wings were wet from the rain and snow. The ants said, "We're sorry. If you had told us, we would have worked harder and saved some food for you, but now it is too late. If we lend you food, there will not be enough food for us. Sorry, very sorry." Then they closed their door.

7   The next day, when the ants opened their door, they found the cicadas dead. That's why, nowadays, we can hear cicadas sing in the summer, but not in the winter.

COMPREHENSION

Answer the following questions in pairs or small groups.

1. "If you don't do the same thing, you'll be sorry later!" What do the ants want the cicadas to do?

2. "If you had told us, we would have worked harder." What should the cicadas have told the ants?

3. "Now it is too late." What is it too late for?

4. "We can hear the cicadas sing in the summer, but not in the winter." What doesn't happen in the winter?

VOCABULARY

1 *Match the words in the first column with their definitions in the second column.*

1. _____ industrious		**a.**	in present times
2. _____ preparing		**b.**	cold
3. _____ invited		**c.**	asked someone to go somewhere or do something
4. _____ to join		**d.**	to come together
5. _____ chilly		**e.**	getting ready
6. _____ nowadays		**f.**	hardworking

2 *Match the words in the first column with the words that mean the opposite, their* **antonyms**, *in the second column. The first one is done for you.*

1. _c_ industrious		**a.**	summer
2. _____ winter		**b.**	borrow
3. _____ damp		**c.**	lazy
4. _____ lend		**d.**	alive
5. _____ dead		**e.**	dry

3 The suffix (ending) *-ous* is an adjective ending meaning "full of" or "having a lot of." Note that in words ending in *-y* preceded by a consonant, *y* becomes *i* before adding *-ous*.

Examples: joy   *joyous*
marvel   *marvelous*
industry   *industrious*

*Write examples of adjectives ending with -**ous**. Compare your answers with a partner.*

_____

GRAMMAR

The word *when* is used to combine sentences when a specific time, day, week, season, and so on, is mentioned. The word *where* is used to combine sentences when a specific place is mentioned. Be sure to put the *when* clause after the time word and to put the *where* clause after the place word.

Examples: The ants prepared for the winter. They would have to stay inside then.

The ants prepared for the winter, when they would have to stay inside. (Notice that the word *then* is not used in the combined sentence, and a comma is added.)

The ants stayed in the anthill. It was dry there.
The ants stayed in the anthill, where it was dry. (Notice that the word *there* is not used in the combined sentence, and a comma is added.)

Combine each pair of sentences using **when** *or* **where** *after the underlined word.*

1. My favorite season is the <u>summer</u>. It is warm then.

_____

2. The cicadas do not like <u>winter</u>. It is cold and wet then.

_____

3. The cicadas flew to the <u>farm</u>. The food was good there.

_____

4. The cicadas played <u>outside</u>. It was warm there.

_____

5. The cicadas came to the <u>anthill</u>. The ants lived there.

_____

With a partner, write three sentences that are combined with **when** *or* **where** *clauses.*

_____

_____

_____

PRONUNCIATION AND SPELLING

The letter *c* has two different sounds in the word *cicada*. It also has two different sounds in the words *circle*, *circus*, and *circumference*.

> *c* + *i* or *e* is pronounced *s*.
> *c* + *a*, *o*, *u*, or a consonant is pronounced *k*.

*Write words with the letter **c**.*

1. Write five words in which *c* is pronounced as *s*.

   _____

2. Write five words in which *c* is pronounced as *k*.

   _____

3. Write other words that contain both pronunciations of *c*.

   _____

DISCUSSION AND WRITING

Discuss or write answers to these questions.

1. Do you think the ants should have given food to the cicadas? Why or why not?

2. There is a saying in English "Make hay while the sun shines." It means "Do work outside while the weather is good." What does this saying have to do with the story?

3. Stories like this one teach a lesson, or moral. What do you think the lesson is?

4. Some stories explain a fact about nature. What did you learn from this story about when you can hear cicadas and when you can't hear them?

5. Tell another story you know that teaches a lesson similar to this one.

JUST FOR FUN

1. Retell the story using the pictures on page 20.

2. Work in small groups to act out a scene from the story. The rest of the class must guess which scene it is.

Chapter 4

Señor Billy Goat

a folktale from Puerto Rico

BEFORE YOU READ A and B

1. Look at the picture of the vegetable garden. Which of these vegetables do you know? Which have you eaten? Which of them are popular in your country?

2. If a hungry animal got into your garden, how could you make it go away?

Señor is a Spanish word that means *"mister."* It is pronounced *"senyour."*

1. Read to the end of paragraph 2. What do you think the old man saw in his garden?

2. Read to the end of paragraph 4. What do you think the ant will do? Then continue reading to see if you were right.

■ ■ ■

Señor Billy Goat

1   Once upon a time, a little old man and a little old woman lived in the hills of Puerto Rico. In their garden, they grew many vegetables such as tomatoes, pumpkins, potatoes, beans, and corn. They spent many hours working in the garden.

2   Every morning, while the wife made coffee, the old man looked out the window at his beautiful garden. But one day he saw something in the garden. "Maria, come quickly," he called to his wife. "Something is eating our vegetables."

3   He went out to the garden and saw that it was a billy goat. "Please don't eat up the garden, Señor Billy Goat! We are old and we need our vegetables," he said. But the goat turned his horns toward the old man and made him run away.

4   The old man and his wife started to cry. Just then a little black ant fell into the man's hand. "What will you give me if I help you?" asked the ant. "I can make the goat go away." They promised her a little bag of flour and a little bag of sugar, and she went away.

5   The ant went to the garden. She walked up the goat's leg, over his back, and up to his ear. Then she stung him. "Ouch," cried the goat. Then the ant began to sting the goat on his ears, legs, and back.

6   "I must have stepped on an anthill!" the billy goat said, and he ran out of the garden. He rolled on the ground to try to kill the ant. But he forgot that he was on a hill. So he rolled down, down, down. Maybe he is still rolling!

7   The man and his wife were happy. They gave the ant a bag of flour and one of sugar, as they had promised. After that, they never had problems with goats.

COMPREHENSION

1 *Write **T** next to the sentences that are **true**. Write **F** next to the sentences that are **false**.*

1. _____ The old man was unhappy to see the goat.

2. _____ The goat saw the ant coming.

3. _____ The goat wasn't hungry.

4. _____ The old man paid the ant for her help.

5. _____ At first the old man tried to talk to the goat.

2 *Number the sentences to show the correct story order.*

_____ The man and his wife started to cry.

_____ The goat rolled down, down, down.

_____ The old man saw something in his garden.

_____ The ant stung the goat.

_____ The old man asked the goat not to eat the vegetables in the garden.

_____ The ant said that she could make the goat go away.

VOCABULARY

1 *Complete the sentences with words from the list.*

garden	horns	stung
make	quickly	pumpkins
spent	still	promised

1. The goat pushed the old man with his _____ .

2. The old man and the old woman _____ to give flour and sugar to the ant.

3. From their _____ , they got food to eat and sell.

4. They grew _____ in their garden.

5. A bee _____ the boy on his arm.

6. I have looked for the book for two weeks, but I _____ haven't found it.

7. Maria's parents _____ her wash the dishes every night.

8. He _____ last summer at his family's farm.

9. Don't run too _____ . You might fall.

Circle the word in each row that is different from the others. Use your dictionary if you need help.

1. chicken   goat   pumpkin   rabbit   turtle

2. apples   corn   potatoes   beans   spinach

3. roll   fall   grow   wife   walk

4. ant   fly   cicada   sugar   mosquito

GRAMMAR

Look back at the story. Find the sentence in the paragraph shown in parentheses. Then, write who or what the underlined pronouns refer to.

1. <u>They</u> promised <u>her</u> a little bag of flour . . . (paragraph 4)

   they _____

   her _____

2. Then <u>she</u> stung <u>him</u>. (paragraph 5)

   she _____

   him _____

3. Maybe <u>he</u> is still rolling! (paragraph 6)

   he _____

4. After that, <u>they</u> never had problems with goats. (paragraph 7)

   they _____

B WHILE YOU READ

1. Read to the end of paragraph 2. What do you think the old man saw in his garden?

2. Read to the end of paragraph 4. What do you think the ant will do? Then continue reading to see if you were right.

Señor Billy Goat

1   Once upon a time, an old couple lived in the highlands of Puerto Rico. They had a garden where they grew many crops such as tomatoes, pumpkins, potatoes, beans, and corn.

2   Every morning while his wife prepared the coffee, the old man looked out the window at his beautiful garden. One day, the man thought he saw something digging in his garden.

3   He went outside to check, and sure enough, there was a billy goat in the garden. He begged the billy goat to go away, but the goat refused to leave.

4   The old couple began to cry, but a little ant said that she would help them in exchange for one tiny sack of flour and one of sugar.

5   The ant went to the garden and started to crawl all over the billy goat. "Ouch!" cried the goat, as the little ant began to sting him. "I must have stepped on an anthill!" he cried, running out of the garden.

6   He tried to get rid of the ant by rolling on the ground. But he forgot that he was on a hill, so he rolled down, down, down. Perhaps he's still rolling!

7   Of course, the old man and the old woman were happy. They gave flour and sugar to the ant as they had promised. They never saw the billy goat again. And they lived happily ever after.

COMPREHENSION

Answer the following questions in pairs or small groups.

1. What crops did the old man grow?
2. What phrase tells you that this story took place long ago?
3. Why did the ant offer her help?
4. What happened to the goat?
5. What did the old man give the ant for her help?

VOCABULARY

Match the words in the first column with their definitions in the second column.

1. _____ a couple
2. _____ crops
3. _____ prepared
4. _____ begged
5. _____ refused
6. _____ to exchange
7. _____ tiny
8. _____ a sack
9. _____ to get rid of

a. plants grown to eat or use
b. said "no"
c. to trade one thing for another
d. a bag
e. to make go away
f. asked for very strongly
g. very small
h. a husband and wife or any two people in love
i. got ready

DICTIONARY SKILLS

Use your dictionary to find the definition and part of speech for each underlined word as it is used in the sentence. The first one is done for you.

1. They grew many <u>crops</u> in their garden.

    definition ___plants grown on a farm or in a garden to eat or use___

    part of speech ___noun___

2. They gave the ant a <u>sack</u> of flour.

    definition _____

    part of speech _____

3. The goat <u>rolled</u> on the ground.

definition _____

part of speech _____

4. The goat rolled on the <u>ground</u>.

definition _____

part of speech _____

5. The old man went outside to <u>check</u>.

definition _____

part of speech _____

GRAMMAR

1 *Look back at the story. Find the sentence in the paragraph shown in parentheses. Then, write who or what the underlined words refer to.*

1. The old couple began to cry, but a little ant said that <u>she</u> would help <u>them</u> . . . (paragraph 4)

she _____

them _____

2. . . . a little ant said that she would help them in exchange for one tiny sack of flour and <u>one</u> of sugar. (paragraph 4)

one _____

2 *Combine each pair of sentences using the word* **one** *to make one sentence with the same meaning. The first one is done for you.*

1. He gave her a sack of flour. He gave her a sack of sugar.

<u>He gave her a sack of flour and one of sugar.</u> _____

2. Sally gave him a box of cereal. She gave him a box of cookies.

_____

3. Mike bought three cans of blue paint. He bought one can of red paint.

_____

4. Please get two quarts of orange juice. Get one quart of milk.

_____

3 *Combine each pair of sentences using the* **-ing** *verb form to make one sentence with the same meaning. The first one is done for you.*

1. He saw the goat. It was digging in the garden.

   <u>He saw the goat digging in the garden.</u>

2. She heard her husband. He was calling her.

   _____

3. The cicadas saw the ants. They were carrying food.

   _____

4. The girl saw an old man. He was sharpening a piece of iron.

   _____

DISCUSSION AND WRITING

Discuss or write answers to these questions.

1. Many stories in English begin with the phrase *Once upon a time . . .* When we see *once upon a time . . . ,* we know that we are going to read about something that happened a long time ago. We also know that the story is not usually true. There are also other ways to start a story. Look at the first lines of other stories in this book. What other beginning phrases do you see?

2. *And they lived happily ever after* is often used to end stories in English. How do stories usually begin and end in your country?

3. Ants appeared in two stories, "The Ant and the Cicada" and "Señor Billy Goat." What did these two stories teach about ants?

4. In this story, a very small animal tricks a much larger, stronger animal. Look at the following list of characters. Can you think of similar stories with these characters?

   - a younger brother and an older brother
   - a young boy and a giant
   - a poor young girl and her rich older sisters
   - a smart, small animal and a big, powerful animal

5. According to this story, what crops grow in Puerto Rico? What crops grow in your country?

6. *Get rid of* means "make something go away." Did you ever have pests (annoying animals or insects) in your house? How did you get rid of them?

JUST FOR FUN

1. Read this story from Mexico, which is similar to "Señor Billy Goat." In pairs, make a list of the similarities and differences between the two stories.

The Ram in the Chili Patch

Juan was a hardworking Mexican boy. He helped raise money for his family by growing chili peppers in his garden. But one day when he came out to his chili patch, he found a ram there eating some peppers and stomping on others. "Go away, Mr. Ram," said Juan. "Those are my peppers. "The ram replied, "Get away from me or I'll butt you into the next county." Juan started to cry, and all the animals on the little farm felt sorry for him. The cat tried to help. She went up to the ram and said, "You should be ashamed of yourself. Get out of there. Those are Juan's chili peppers." But the ram lowered his head and said, "Get out of here or I'll butt you into the next county." So the cat ran away. The dog tried to help. He came out and barked at the ram, but the ram lowered his head and said, "Get out of here or I'll butt you into the next county." The dog too ran away. Finally a little ant said, "I can help you, Juan." The ant climbed onto the ram and began biting him all over. The ram jumped up and started running. He ran so fast and so far that now he is in the next county!

2. Act out the story "The Ram in the Chili Patch."

Chapter 5

The Mountain God and the River God

a folktale from Vietnam

BEFORE YOU READ A and B

1. Look at the picture. Who is this woman? How do you know?

2. What do you think is the best way to find someone to love or marry?

WHILE YOU READ

1. Where is the woman in the picture on page 38? Why is she there?

2. What natural event is explained in this story?

3. Read to the end of paragraph 3. What do you think will happen next?

The Mountain God and the River God

1 A long time ago in Vietnam, there was a beautiful princess. She was the king's only daughter.

2 Both the mountain god and the river god wanted to marry the king's daughter. The king said, "You must fight, and the winner will marry the princess."

3 So the two gods fought. They fought with bows and arrows. The mountain god won the fight, and he married the beautiful princess.

4 But the river god was angry. He used his power to attack the mountain. The river got higher. It covered the mountain. It came up to where the mountain god and the princess lived. Then, the mountain god used his power. The mountain got higher too, so the river couldn't get the princess.

5 Now every year in July and August, when the rains come in Vietnam, and the rivers rise, people say that the river god is still trying to take away the princess.

COMPREHENSION

1 *Write* **T** *next to the sentences that are* **true**. *Write* **F** *next to the sentences that are* **false**.

1. _____ The king married the mountain god.

2. _____ The princess married the mountain god.

3. _____ The two gods fought with guns.

4. _____ The mountain god won the fight.

5. _____ The rivers in Vietnam rise in July and August.

6. _____ The river god was angry after the fight.

7. _____ Both gods wanted to marry the princess.

8. _____ The mountain got higher.

9. _____ The river got so high that it got the princess.

10. _____ The princess was the king's only daughter.

2 *Number the sentences to show the correct story order.*

_____ The river god was angry.

_____ The two gods wanted to marry the princess.

_____ The river got higher.

_____ The mountain god won the fight.

_____ The mountain got higher.

_____ The mountain god and the river god had a fight.

3 *Answer the following questions in pairs or small groups.*

1. Where does this story take place?

2. Which god won the fight?

3. What weapon (tool for fighting) did the gods use?

4. What natural event does this story explain?

5. Who decided which god the princess would marry? How was this decided?

VOCABULARY

Complete the sentences with words or phrases from the list.

| attack | bow and arrow | mountain |
| princess | river | power |

1. The daughter of a king is a _____ .

2. A very high hill is called a _____ .

3. The hunter used a _____ to kill animals.

4. The mountain god was very strong. He had a lot of _____ .

5. Soldiers sometimes _____ their enemies.

GRAMMAR

1 *Look back at the story. Find the sentence in the paragraph shown in parentheses. Then, write who or what the underlined pronouns refer to.*

1. The king said, "You must fight . . . (paragraph 2)

you _____

2. He used his power to attack the mountain. (paragraph 4)

he _____

his _____

3. It covered the mountain. (paragraph 4)

it _____

2 *Complete the sentences with the correct verb forms.*

rise	rises	rising	rose

1. Every summer the river _____ .

2. The water in the lake is _____ because of the rain.

3. The water _____ so high that it caused a flood.

4. Does the river always _____ in the summer?

PRONUNCIATION AND SPELLING

1 *Say each word aloud or repeat after your teacher. Then, circle the words in which* **gh** *sounds like* **f**.

fought   tough   caught   laugh   rough

1. Sometimes *gh* is silent as in *fought, caught,* or *taught.* Write other words in which *gh* is silent. Share your list with a partner.

_____

2. Sometimes *gh* sounds like *f* as in *tough, laugh,* or *rough.* Write other words in which *gh* sounds like *f.* Share your list with a partner.

_____

2 *Say each word aloud or repeat after your teacher. Then, circle the words in which **ow** sounds like **o**.*

2
*Say each word aloud or repeat after your teacher. Then, circle the words in which **ow** sounds like **o**.*

snow   cow   low   flower   now

1. Sometimes *ow* sounds like *o* as in *bow* (weapon or hair ribbon) or *low*. Write other words in which *ow* is pronounced *o*. Share your list with a partner.

_____

2. Sometimes *ow* is pronounced *ou* as in *bow* (bend at the waist), *flower*, or *cow*. Write other words in which *ow* sounds like *ou*. Share your list with a partner.

_____

B

WHILE YOU READ

1. Where is the woman in the picture on page 38? Why is she there?

2. What natural event is explained in this story?

3. Read to the end of paragraph 3. What do you think will happen next?

■ ■ ■

The Mountain God and the River God

1   Once upon a time in the days of King Hung Vuong in Vietnam, there was a beautiful princess. She was the king's only daughter.

2   Both the river god and the mountain god came to the king. Each wanted to ask for the hand of his only daughter. But the king told them that they had to first fight each other, and the winner could marry the princess.

3   So the two gods had a contest with bows and arrows. The mountain god won, and he married the beautiful princess.

4   But the river god was angry. He attacked the mountain with all his might. He made the river rise and flow around the mountain. Soon it almost reached the princess! Then, in response, the mountain rose, too, so the water couldn't reach the princess.

5   That was many years ago. But even today in July and August, when the rains come in Vietnam, and the rivers rise, people remember the rivalry between the two gods. The people say that the river god is still trying to take away the princess.

COMPREHENSION

Answer the following questions in pairs or small groups.

1. Why did the mountain god and the river god go to see King Hung Vuong?

2. Who decided whom the princess would marry? How was it decided?

3. Who married the princess? Why?

4. What did the river god do after the contest? Why did he do it?

5. What natural event does this story explain?

VOCABULARY

1. Match the words in the first column with the words that mean the opposite in the second column.

1. _____ a king
2. _____ a daughter
3. _____ a winner
4. _____ angry
5. _____ rose
6. _____ to remember
7. _____ a rivalry

a. fell
b. a friendship
c. to forget
d. happy
e. a loser
f. a queen
g. a son

2. Three of the words or phrases in each of these rows have almost the same meaning. Circle the word or phrase that has a different meaning. Use your dictionary if you need help.

1. might   power   strength   persistence
2. rivalry   friendship   competition   contest
3. rise   go up   get higher   respond

Complete the sentences with words or phrases from the list.

attacked	flow	bow and arrow	contest	to ask for the hand of

1. In the past when a man wanted to marry a girl, he went to her father
   _____ his daughter.

2. They had a _____ to decide who was stronger.

3. Does the river always _____ over its banks after a heavy rain?

4. The soldier _____ his enemy with a _____ .

DICTIONARY SKILLS

Use your dictionary to find the definition and part of speech for each underlined word as it is used in the sentence.

1. She put a yellow <u>bow</u> in her hair.

   definition _____

   part of speech _____

2. The hunter shot the animal with a <u>bow</u> and arrow.

   definition _____

   part of speech _____

3. The man had to <u>bow</u> when the king passed by.

   definition _____

   part of speech _____

4. The gods fought with all their <u>might</u>.

   definition _____

   part of speech _____

5. If the river gets high enough, the princess <u>might</u> drown.

   definition _____

   part of speech _____

6. The water level <u>rose</u> dangerously.

   definition _____

   part of speech _____

7. The prince brought the princess a <u>rose</u>.

definition _____

part of speech _____

8. She wore a <u>rose</u>-colored dress.

definition _____

part of speech _____

9. The mountain god won the <u>contest</u>.

definition _____

part of speech _____

10. The river god wanted to <u>contest</u> the results of the competition.

definition _____

part of speech _____

GRAMMAR

1 *Combine each pair of sentences using* **both . . . and** *to make one sentence with the same meaning. The first one is done for you.*

1. The river god wanted to marry the princess. The mountain god wanted to marry the princess. <u>Both the river god and the mountain god wanted to marry the princess.</u>

2. The river god had magic powers. The mountain god had magic powers.

_____

_____

3. The river got higher. The mountain got higher.

_____

_____

2 *Combine each pair of sentences using the word in parentheses to make one sentence with the same meaning. Remember to add a comma.*

1. The river god was angry. He attacked the mountain.

   (so) *The river god was angry, so he attacked the mountain.*

2. Each wanted to marry the princess. The king told them they had to fight.

   (but) _____

3. They had to fight each other. The winner could marry the princess.

   (and) _____

DISCUSSION AND WRITING

Discuss or write answers to these questions.

1. How do you feel about the behavior of the river god? Would you have behaved the same way in his place? Why or why not?

2. In your opinion, is it better to choose your own spouse (husband or wife) or have your family choose for you? What are the good and bad points of making the choice yourself? What are the good and bad points of having your family choose for you?

3. Pretend that the river god is telling the story. Retell paragraphs 2, 3, and 4. Start with the sentences, *Both the mountain god and I came to the king. Both of us wanted to ask for the hand of the king's only daughter.*

JUST FOR FUN A and B

1. Work in two groups and have a debate. One side will argue for choosing one's own spouse. The other side will argue for having a parent or someone else choose the spouse. Use your answer to Discussion and Writing, question 2, for help.

2. Tell a story from your country that explains the reason for rain, snow, floods, or other natural events.

Chapter 6

The Golden Touch

a folktale from the Middle East

BEFORE YOU READ A and B

1. Did you ever wish for something and then feel sorry when your wish came true?

2. Did you ever wish that you were rich? What would you do if you were suddenly rich?

3. What are the advantages of having everything you touch turn to gold? What are the disadvantages?

4. Look at the pictures. What do you know about the man in picture 1? Who do you think the little girl is?

5. Is the king happy or upset in picture 5? How do you know?

WHILE YOU READ

1. Read to the end of paragraph 2. What do you think will happen when the king gets his wish? Will he be happy or sorry? Continue reading to see if you were right.

2. Read to the end of paragraph 4. What do you think will happen next? Continue reading to see if you were right.

■ ■ ■

The Golden Touch

1   There once was a king. He was very rich. The king loved two things: his little daughter and his gold. He had many rooms full of gold, but he was not happy. He wanted to have more gold.

2   One day the king was in his garden. A strange man came to see him. The stranger told the king to make a wish. The king said, "I wish to have more gold." "I will help you get your wish," the stranger answered. "Tomorrow morning, everything you touch will change to gold."

3   The next morning the king got up early. He touched a chair, a flower, and a table. Everything changed to gold! The king was very happy. He sat down to eat his breakfast, but his food turned to gold when he touched it. He thought, "If I can't eat anything, I will die."

4   Then his little daughter came into the room. She ran to her father. But when he touched her, she changed to gold, too.

5   The king was very sad. He walked alone in his garden. Then he saw the stranger again. "Oh," cried the king, "please take back my wish. I don't want any more gold." "All right," said the stranger, "if you are really sure this time, I will take back your wish."

6   After that, the king was not as rich, but he was wiser and happier.

COMPREHENSION

1 *Write **T** next to the sentences that are **true**. Write **F** next to the sentences that are **false**.*

1. _____ The king was happy because he had so much gold.

2. _____ The king loved gold more than he loved his daughter.

3. _____ If the king had kept "the golden touch" for a long time, he would have died.

4. _____ The king was very happy with "the golden touch."

5. _____ The king didn't want to keep "the golden touch."

2 *Number the sentences to show the correct story order.*

_____ The king's daughter turned to gold.

_____ The king asked for more gold.

_____ The king asked the stranger to take back the wish.

_____ A chair turned to gold.

_____ The king's food turned to gold.

_____ The king was wiser and happier.

_____ The stranger said, "Everything you touch will change to gold."

3 *Answer the following questions in pairs or small groups.*

1. What two things did the king love? Which one do you think he loved more? How do you know?

2. Why wasn't the king happy at the beginning of the story?

3. How did the king get "the golden touch"?

4. When did the king first know that "the golden touch" was a problem?

5. Why wasn't the king happy after he got his wish?

6. *After that, the king was not as rich, but he was wiser and happier.* (paragraph 6). What does *after that* refer to?

VOCABULARY

1 *Complete the sentences with words from the list.*

change	daughter	stranger	touch	wiser

1. That bowl can break easily, so please don't _____ it.

2. Anna has two children, a son and a _____.

3. He was a _____ in that town, so he didn't know where to go.

4. When people grow up, they often _____; they don't stay exactly the same.

5. Older people are sometimes _____ than younger people.

2 *Circle the word in each row that means the opposite of the first word.*

1. **happy**   glad   tired   sad   mean
2. **give**   ask for   lend   take back   want
3. **rich**   money   poor   wealthy   important
4. **wise**   stupid   smart   rude   unhappy
5. **stranger**   visitor   friend   king   daughter

GRAMMAR

The word *too* means "more than is good, acceptable, or necessary."
The word *very* means "much" or "a lot."

Examples:

The king liked gold <u>very</u> much. After he got "the golden touch," he realized that he had liked gold <u>too</u> much.

She likes her bath water <u>very</u> hot. But if the water is <u>too</u> hot, she could get burned.

Children like to eat candy <u>very</u> much. But if they eat <u>too</u> much candy, they may ruin their teeth.

Write **too** *or* **very** *in the following sentences.*

1. John loves his girlfriend _____ much, so he is going to ask her to marry him.

2. Because Jane spends _____ much time with her boyfriend, her grades in school are bad.

3. If people spend _____ much time in the sun, they can get sunburned.

4. She liked her birthday present _____ much.

WHILE YOU READ

1. Read to the end of paragraph 2. What do you think will happen when the king gets his wish? Will he be happy or sorry? Continue reading to see if you were right.

2. Read to the end of paragraph 4. What do you think will happen next? Continue reading to see if you were right.

■ ■ ■

The Golden Touch

1 There once lived a king named Midas who was very rich. He loved two things above all else: his little daughter and his gold. The king had many rooms full of gold, but he wasn't satisfied. He wanted to possess even more gold.

2 One day when the king was in his garden, an unknown visitor came to him. He told the king that he could wish for anything he wanted. At first the king did not believe the stranger, but finally he was convinced. "I wish to have more gold," the king said. "Very well," answered the stranger. "You shall have your wish. Beginning tomorrow, everything you touch will turn to gold."

3 The next morning the king got out of bed early. He wanted to see if his wish had been granted. First, he touched a chair, then a flower, then a table. Everything he touched turned to gold! The king was very happy. Then, he sat down to eat breakfast. But as soon as he touched his food, it turned to gold. The king began to worry. What would happen if he couldn't eat anything?

4 Just then the little princess came into the dining room. She ran to her father. But as he touched her, she turned to gold.

5 The king was sad and worried. He went out to the garden. As he was walking, he saw the stranger again. The king begged him to take back the wish. "I don't want any more gold," he cried. The stranger warned the king to be absolutely sure this time. Then, he agreed to take back the wish.

6 From that day on, the king was a wiser and happier man, even though he had less gold.

COMPREHENSION

Answer the following questions in pairs or small groups.

1. Look back at the story "A Wise Wish" on page 16. How are these two stories alike? How are they different?

2. When did the king realize that "the golden touch" was a problem?

3. Why do you think this story is called "The Golden Touch"?

VOCABULARY

Match the words in the first column with their definitions in the second column.

1. ____ to possess   **a.** starting

2. ____ unknown   **b.** to own

3. ____ a stranger   **c.** someone you don't know

4. ____ convinced   **d.** after that time

5. ____ beginning   **e.** unfamiliar, strange

6. ____ granted   **f.** to be nervous, upset

7. ____ to worry   **g.** gave

8. ____ warned   **h.** made someone believe something

9. ____ absolutely   **i.** completely, definitely

10. ____ from that day on   **j.** cautioned

DICTIONARY SKILLS

Use your dictionary to find the definition and part of speech for each underlined word as it is used in the sentence.

1. Some students get <u>grants</u> to go to college.

   definition _____

   parts of speech _____

2. The Sunshine Foundation <u>grants</u> the wishes of sick children.

   definition _____

   part of speech _____

3. Don't let that man inside. He is a <u>stranger</u>.

definition _____

part of speech _____

4. Sometimes truth is <u>stranger</u> than fiction.

definition _____

part of speech _____

GRAMMAR

1 *Combine each pair of sentences by putting the adjective from the second sentence into the first sentence. The first one is done for you.*

1. There was a king. He was rich.

<u>There was a rich king.</u>

2. He had a daughter. She was little.

_____

3. The king made a wish. His wish was foolish.

_____

2 Most one-syllable and some two-syllable adjectives add *–er* to make the comparative form.

Example: tall   *taller*   quiet   *quieter*

Words ending in *–e* add *–r* to form the comparative.

Example: nice   *nicer*

Words ending in *–y* preceded by a consonant change the *y* to *i* before adding *–er*.

Example: pretty   *prettier*

Write the comparative form for the following adjectives. The first one is done for you.

1. wise   <u>*wiser*</u>

2. safe   _____

3. happy   _____

4. rich   _____

On a separate piece of paper, write sentences using each of the new adjectives.

DISCUSSION AND WRITING [A and B]

Discuss or write the answers to these questions.

1. To have "the Midas touch" or "the golden touch" means that a person makes a lot of money in business. Describe someone you know who has "the Midas touch."

2. Tell a story about someone who got what he or she wished for and was sorry later.

3. What do you think the king's life was like after the story? Do you think he was sorry that he gave back his wish?

4. Does this story tell us anything about how people can act? Is the king like anyone you have ever met?

5. Pretend the king is telling the story. Retell paragraphs 2 and 3. Start with the sentence *One day when I was in my garden, an unknown visitor came to see me.*

JUST FOR FUN [A and B]

1. Use the pictures on page 47 to retell the story in your own words.

2. Find the following words in the puzzle. The words can be written across, up and down, forward, or backward.

daughter	touch	king	stranger	Midas
satisfied	golden	possess	wish	princess

```
d  a  u  g  h  t  e  r
e  m  w  o  v  o  x  e
i  i  i  l  d  u  a  g
f  d  s  d  e  c  n  n
s  a  h  e  b  h  m  a
i  s  c  n  p  s  w  r
t  k  i  n  g  b  i  t
a  p  o  s  s  e  s  s
s  s  e  c  n  i  r  p
```

Chapter 7

Ritva's Quilt

a folktale from Finland

BEFORE YOU READ A and B

1. What is a quilt? How is it made?

2. Look at the pictures. What does the man think of the quilt? Is it too small or too big?

3. What would you do if something you made was too small or too big?

WHILE YOU READ

1. Read to the end of paragraph 1. Do you expect this story to be sad? Silly? Serious? Why?

2. Read to the end of paragraph 5. How do you expect Ritva to solve this problem?

■ ■ ■

Ritva's Quilt

1   Long ago in the far north, there was a small town that everyone knew about. This town was famous because its people were very kind but not very smart.

2   In this small town, a good man and woman lived in their little house. The wife, Ritva, was making a fine patch quilt for her husband, Kalle. Patches are pieces of cloth and wool of different colors. She sewed the pieces together to make a quilt, which is a blanket made of many patches.

3   Ritva was very happy with the quilt when it was finished. She called all her neighbors to come and look at it. Everyone agreed that it was beautiful. "Ritva, my dear," said Kalle, "I am so lucky. You were very smart to make such a wonderful quilt. It is beautiful!"

4   That night when they went to sleep, Kalle covered himself with the new quilt. It was a cold night, so Kalle pulled the quilt over his ears. But when he did, his feet were out in the cold. The quilt was too short.

5   In the morning Kalle said, "Dear wife, the beautiful quilt that you made for me is too short. Every time I pull it over my ears, it uncovers my feet, and they get cold." Then Ritva said, "Good husband, did you say the quilt covered your ears but not your feet?" "That's right. My neck and ears were covered and warm, but my feet were cold. It's too short at the feet."

6   After breakfast, Ritva took her scissors and cut off a wide piece from the top of the quilt. Then she sewed it to the other end. "Now," she said, "this will take care of Kalle's feet."

7   That night, Kalle used the new quilt again. But after he covered his neck and ears and face, his feet were out in the cold, just like the night before. The next morning he told Ritva. "Maybe I should cut off more at the neck," she said.

8   So again, she cut off a wide piece at the top end and sewed it to the bottom end. But of course, that did not help.

9   Ritva continued to cut at one end of the quilt and sew to the other end. Finally, she grew tired and decided it would be best to make a new quilt. Both Ritva and Kalle hoped the new one would be long enough!

COMPREHENSION

1 *Find the paragraph that gives the information in each sentence. Do this exercise as quickly as you can; then discuss your answers in pairs or small groups. The first one is done for you.*

1. People came to admire the new quilt.

   paragraph __3__

2. Ritva decided to fix the problem.

   paragraph _____

3. People had opinions about Ritva and Kalle's town.

   paragraph _____

4. Ritva gave up trying to fix the quilt.

   paragraph _____

5. Kalle's new quilt had a problem.

   paragraph _____

2 *Reread paragraphs 2, 3, 5, and 7. Find one sentence that best expresses the main idea of each paragraph. Discuss your answers in pairs or small groups. The first one is done for you.*

1. paragraph 2 <u>The wife, Ritva, was making a fine patch quilt for her husband, Kalle.</u>

2. paragraph 3 _____

3. paragraph 5 _____

4. paragraph 7 _____

3 *Answer the following questions in pairs or small groups.*

1. What did Ritva make for Kalle?

2. How did she make it?

3. What was the problem with the quilt?

4. How did Ritva try to fix the problem?

5. Was the quilt ever fixed?

VOCABULARY

Find a word in the story that means the opposite of each of the following words. Use your dictionary if you need help. The first one is done for you.

1. beginning   _____ *end* _____

2. narrow   _____

3. started   _____

4. huge   _____

5. ugly   _____

6. unknown   _____

7. stupid   _____

GRAMMAR

The words **a**, **an**, and **the** are **articles**. Complete the sentences with the correct article. Then, check the story to see if your answer is correct. The first one is done for you.

1. Ritva was making __a__ fine patch quilt for her husband.

2. She sewed _____ pieces together.

3. Kalle covered himself with _____ new quilt.

4. _____ quilt was too short.

5. So again, she cut off _____ wide piece at the top end and sewed it to the bottom end.

6. Finally, she grew tired and decided it would be best to make _____ new quilt.

WHILE YOU READ

1. Read to the end of paragraph 1. Do you expect this story to be sad? Silly? Serious? Why?

2. Read to the end of paragraph 5. How do you expect Ritva to solve this problem?

Ritva's Quilt

1   Once upon a time in the far north, there was a small town whose people had a reputation for being very kind but not very intelligent. During the long winter evenings, people who lived nearby often sat by their fires and told stories about what happened there.

2   In this town lived a happy couple in a tiny house. One day, Ritva, the wife, decided to make a fine patch quilt for her husband, Kalle. To make the quilt, she sewed together many pieces of cloth of different patterns and colors.

3   When she finished, Ritva was very pleased with the result. She invited her neighbors to come and see her work. Everyone admired it. Kalle was especially happy. He told her how beautiful the quilt was and how much he appreciated it.

4   When Kalle went to sleep that night, he covered himself with the new quilt. The night was cold, so he pulled it up over his ears. But as soon as he did that, his feet were uncovered because the quilt was too short!

5   In the morning, Kalle told Ritva what had happened. "When I pull the cover over my ears, my feet get cold." "Good husband," Ritva said, "did you say the quilt covered your ears but not your feet?" "That's right," he replied. "My neck and ears were warm, but my feet were cold. It's too short at the feet."

6   That morning, Ritva took her scissors and cut off a wide strip from the top of the quilt and sewed it onto the bottom. "Now your feet will be nice and warm," she said.

7   That night when he went to sleep, Kalle again used the new quilt. But after he covered his neck and ears and face, his feet were cold, just like the night before. The next morning he explained this to Ritva. "Perhaps I need to cut more off the top," she thought.

8   So she cut another wide strip from the top and stitched it to the bottom of the quilt. But of course, that did not solve the problem!

9   Ritva kept cutting at one end and adding to the other end. Finally she gave up and decided to make Kalle a new quilt. They both hoped it would be long enough this time!

COMPREHENSION

*Write **T** next to the sentences that are **true** and **F** next to the sentences that are **false**. Write **X** if the story doesn't give this information.*

1. _____ Ritva was pleased with the quilt she made for Kalle.

2. _____ She tried to fix the quilt only one time.

3. _____ The scissors she used were not very sharp.

4. _____ The neighbors made suggestions about fixing the quilt.

5. _____ Ritva didn't know how to fix the problem.

VOCABULARY

Match the words in the first column with their definitions in the second column.

1. _____ tiny   **a.** extremely small

2. _____ a patch   **b.** was grateful for

3. _____ a quilt   **c.** something that happens because of something else

4. _____ sewed   **d.** a long, narrow piece of cloth or paper

5. _____ patterns   **e.** approved of and respected

6. _____ a result   **f.** people who live near you

7. _____ neighbors   **g.** designs made from shapes, colors, lines, etc.

8. _____ admired   **h.** a warm, thick cover for a bed

9. _____ appreciated   **i.** joined pieces of cloth together using a needle and thread

10. _____ a strip   **j.** a small piece of material, sometimes used to cover a hole

DICTIONARY SKILLS

Use your dictionary to find the definition and part of speech for each underlined word as it is used in the sentence.

1. The people in Ritva's village were very <u>kind</u>.

   definition _____

   part of speech _____

2. What <u>kind</u> of ice cream do you like best?

   definition _____

   part of speech _____

3. Ritva made a <u>cover</u> for her husband.

   definition _____

   part of speech _____

4. The quilt was too short so it didn't <u>cover</u> him completely.

   definition _____

   part of speech _____

5. If you are late for work, I'll <u>cover</u> for you.

   definition _____

   part of speech _____

6. That accident caused a lot of damage to my car, but my insurance will <u>cover</u> it.

   definition _____

   part of speech _____

7. Can you tell me the <u>end</u> of the story?

   definition _____

   part of speech _____

8. She cut material from one <u>end</u> and sewed it onto the other.

   definition _____

   part of speech _____

9. Ritva made a <u>fine</u> quilt for her husband.

   definition _____

   part of speech _____

10. I had to pay a <u>fine</u> because I got a ticket for speeding.

   definition _____

   part of speech _____

GRAMMAR

Look back at the story. Find the sentence in the paragraph shown in parentheses. Then, write who or what the underlined pronouns refer to.

1. When <u>she</u> finished, Ritva was very pleased with the result. (paragraph 3)

   she _____

2. Everyone admired <u>it</u>. (paragraph 3)

   it _____

3. The night was cold, so <u>he</u> pulled <u>it</u> up over his ears. (paragraph 4)

   he _____

   it _____

4. But as soon as <u>he</u> did <u>that</u>, his feet were uncovered . . . (paragraph 4)

   he _____

   that _____

DISCUSSION AND WRITING

Discuss or write answers to these questions.

1. A patch is used to repair something. What can be fixed with a patch?

2. What other stories in this book tell about people who do silly things? Do you know any other stories in English or other languages about people who do silly things?

3. Some people make quilts to tell their family history. They sew pictures of different things that tell about their family. What would be on your family's quilt?

4. What details in this story show that it takes place in the north?

JUST FOR FUN A and B

Act out the story. Use a few simple props (everyday objects such as scissors and a big sheet of paper with a patchwork design drawn on it) to help explain what is going on.

Chapter 8

THE FARMER, THE SON, AND THE DONKEY

BEFORE YOU READ

1. This is a story of a man who gets into trouble because he listens to what other people tell him. Have you ever listened to other people and gotten into trouble?

2. Do you know any stories about a person who has problems selling something? What are they?

3. Look at the picture. Why do you think the man and the boy are carrying the donkey?

1. Read to the end of paragraph 5. What do you think the farmer and his son will do now?

2. Read to the end of paragraph 6. What do you think will happen next?

■ ■ ■

THE FARMER, THE SON, AND THE DONKEY

1   One day, a farmer and his son were walking to town with their donkey. They were going to sell the donkey at the market.

2   On the road, they met some young girls. The girls laughed and said, "Look how foolish they are! Both of them are walking, and one of them could be riding on the donkey." When the farmer heard this, he told his son to get up on the donkey and ride.

3   But soon they passed two men standing near the road. "Look at that!" said one of the men. "That young boy is riding while his poor old father has to walk." So the son got off the donkey, and the farmer got on. They continued down the road toward town.

4   After a short time, they came to some old women standing at a corner. One of them asked the farmer, "How can you let the child walk while you ride? He must be very tired. What kind of father are you?" So the farmer lifted his son up, and both of them rode until they reached the town.

5   When they got to the town, a man saw them and asked, "Is that donkey yours?" "Yes," said the farmer. "You are making that animal work too hard," said the man. You two are better able to carry that donkey than the donkey is to carry you!"

6   The farmer and his son got off the donkey's back. But they did not know how they could carry the animal. They thought and thought. Then the farmer had an idea. He cut a strong stick from a tree. Then he tied the donkey's feet to it with strong rope. He carried one end of the wooden stick, and his son carried the other end.

7   At the town bridge, a crowd of people was standing and watching them. They were laughing, pointing, and talking loudly. The donkey was afraid of all the noise. He began to kick at the ropes. Soon he pulled loose and fell into the water below. The donkey couldn't swim, so he soon drowned.

8   The farmer and his son felt very silly as they started home with no donkey and no money.

Moral: If you try to please everyone, you may not please anyone.

COMPREHENSION

1 *Write **T** next to the statements that are **true**. Write **F** next to the statements that are **false**.*

1. _____ The farmer hoped to get money for his donkey.

2. _____ The townspeople laughed at the father and son carrying the donkey.

3. _____ The donkey didn't like a lot of noise.

4. _____ The father and son couldn't carry the donkey to town.

5. _____ The farmer never changed his mind.

2 *Number the sentences to show the correct story order.*

_____ The townspeople all laughed.

_____ The father and son decided to carry the donkey.

_____ The donkey fell into the water.

_____ The farmer decided to sell the donkey.

_____ The son got off the donkey.

_____ The farmer put his son on the donkey.

VOCABULARY

Match the words in the first column with their definitions in the second column.

1. _____ a donkey
2. _____ foolish
3. _____ both
4. _____ lifted
5. _____ a stick
6. _____ a bridge
7. _____ pointing
8. _____ noise
9. _____ loose
10. _____ drowned
11. _____ a moral
12. _____ to please

a. to make happy

b. silly

c. raised, moved higher

d. died by being under water too long

e. something that connects two sides of a river or a road

f. loud sounds

g. not tied or held tightly

h. a lesson

i. a long, thin piece of wood

j. two people or things together

k. showing something by holding your finger out

l. an animal like a horse used for farm work

GRAMMAR

1 In English, the regular past tense adds *-ed* to the base form of the verb.

Example: look   *looked*

Verbs ending in *-e* add *-d* to form the past tense.

Example: like   *liked*

Verbs ending in *-y* preceded by a consonant change the *y* to *i* before adding *-ed*.

Example: marry   *married*

Write the simple past tense form of these regular verbs. Use your dictionary if you need help. The first one is done for you.

Base	Past	Base	Past
1. laugh	laughed	8. carry	_____
2. pass	_____	9. watch	_____
3. continue	_____	10. point	_____
4. reach	_____	11. pull	_____
5. walk	_____	12. drown	_____
6. lift	_____	13. start	_____
7. tie	_____	14. try	_____

2 *Look back at the story. Find the sentence in the paragraph shown in parentheses. Then, write who or what the underlined pronouns refer to. The first one is done for you.*

1. When the farmer heard <u>this</u>, . . . (paragraph 2)

   <u>"Look how foolish they are! Both of them are walking, and one of them could be riding on the donkey."</u>

2. Look at <u>that</u>! (paragraph 3)

   _____

3. . . . a man saw <u>them</u> . . . (paragraph 5)

   _____

4. <u>They</u> thought and thought. (paragraph 6)

   _____

5. Then he tied the donkey's feet to <u>it</u> with strong rope. (paragraph 6)

   _____

B WHILE YOU READ

1. Read to the end of paragraph 5. What do you think the farmer and his son will do now?

2. Read to the end of paragraph 6. What do you think will happen next?

THE FARMER, THE SON, AND THE DONKEY

1   One day a farmer and his son were on their way to a nearby market town to sell their donkey.

2   As they walked along beside the donkey, they met some young girls on the road. The girls began to laugh at them. "Don't you two look silly!" they said. "Both of you are walking, and one of you could be riding." When the farmer heard this, he agreed. He helped his son up onto the donkey, and they continued on their way.

3   Soon they passed two men standing by the roadside. "Just look at that!" said one. That poor old man is walking while his son rides. The boy ought to be ashamed." So the son got off the donkey, and his father climbed on and rode.

4   They had not gone very far when they came to some old women at a crossroad. One woman scolded the father. "How dare you ride that donkey while that poor child has to walk. He must be exhausted." So the farmer lifted the boy up beside him, and they both rode the rest of the way to town.

5   When they finally arrived in town, they passed a man who wanted to know if the donkey belonged to them. The farmer replied that it was their donkey. "That poor animal is overworked," said the man. "The two of you could carry that beast far better than it can carry you!"

6   So the farmer and his son got down. But they couldn't figure out how to carry the donkey. Finally, the father had an idea. From a tree, he cut a thick branch to make a kind of carrying pole. He tied the donkey's feet to the pole with rope. Then, he and his son each carried one end of the pole with the frightened donkey hanging between them.

7   By the time they reached the bridge, a noisy crowd stood around watching them. The crowd pointed and laughed loudly. All the noise and laughter frightened the donkey. He began to kick and pull at the ropes. Soon he got loose and fell into the river below. Since he couldn't swim, the donkey drowned.

8   The farmer and his son felt very foolish. Slowly they turned and started back home with no donkey and no money.

Moral: If you try to please everyone, you may end up pleasing no one.

COMPREHENSION

1 *Write an **X** next to the sentences that give advice that the farmer followed. The first one is done for you.*

1. __X__ Let your son ride.

2. _____ Ask a good price for the donkey.

3. _____ Make your son walk.

4. _____ Do not sell that donkey.

5. _____ Don't make the donkey work so hard.

2 *Answer the following questions in pairs or small groups.*

1. Why were the farmer and his son going to the market?

2. Why did the boy get on the donkey?

3. What happened when both the boy and his father got on the donkey?

4. Why did the farmer and the boy decide to carry the donkey?

5. How did they carry the donkey?

6. What happened to the donkey?

7. What lesson does this story teach?

VOCABULARY

1 *Match the words in the first column with their definitions in the second column.*

1. _____ ought to   **a.** an animal

2. _____ ashamed   **b.** scared, afraid

3. ___ overworked   **c.** fat, wide; not thin

4. _____ a beast   **d.** a long stick or post

5. _____ thick   **e.** working too much and for too long

6. _____ a branch   **f.** a part of a tree that grows from the trunk

7. _____ a pole   **g.** embarrassed or guilty

8. _____ frightened   **h.** should

2 *Look back at the story. Find the sentence in the paragraph shown in parentheses. Then, find the words that mean the same as the underlined words.*

1. "Don't you two look <u>ridiculous</u>."(paragraph 2)

    ridiculous _____

2. "The boy ought to be <u>embarrassed</u>."(paragraph 3)

    embarrassed _____

3. "The two of you could carry that <u>animal</u> far better than it can carry you." (paragraph 5)

    animal _____

4. He <u>bound</u> the donkey's feet to the pole with rope. (paragraph 6)

    bound _____

5. All the noise and laughter <u>terrified</u> the donkey. (paragraph 7)

    terrified _____

3 *Write the letter of the definition that shows how the word was used in the story. The first one is done for you.*

1. pole ___a___
    a. a long stick or post
    b. the most northern and southern points on the planet
    c. one of two points at the end of a magnet

2. branch _____
    a. a part of a tree that grows out from the trunk
    b. one part of something larger, such as a business
    c. to divide into smaller parts

3. hang _____
    a. to kill someone by dropping them with a rope around their neck
    b. to spend time in a certain place or with certain people
    c. to tie something at the top so the top can't move but the bottom can

4. turn _____
    a. to move or be moved to a different direction
    b. a chance to do something
    c. to move in a circle

5. tie _____

    a. to have the same number of points in a contest

    b. to fasten something with a rope or string

    c. a piece of clothing worn around the neck

6. point _____

    a. the sharp end of something

    b. a position, place, or location

    c. to show something by holding your finger out

DICTIONARY SKILLS

Find each of the following words in the dictionary. Then, look at the top of the dictionary page to find the guide words. Write the guide words next to each word. The first one is done for you. (Note: Your guide words for **foolish** *may be different, depending on the dictionary you use.)*

1. foolish   fluid   forge

2. drown   _____   _____

3. roadside   _____   _____

4. scold   _____   _____

5. laughter   _____   _____

6. continue   _____   _____

7. pole   _____   _____

8. frighten   _____   _____

9. branch   _____   _____

10. ashamed   _____   _____

GRAMMAR

1 *In English, verbs that do not form the simple past by adding -**ed** to the base form are called **irregular verbs**. Write the simple past tense form of these irregular verbs. The first one is done for you. (Hint: Many dictionaries list irregular verbs in a special section in the back.)*

Base	Past
1. make	made
2. tell	_____
3. ride	_____
4. say	_____
5. hear	_____
6. get	_____
7. come	_____
8. is	_____
9. stand	_____
10. let	_____
11. do	_____
12. fall	_____

2 *Write the base form of these simple past tense irregular verbs from the story. The first one is done for you.*

Past	Base
1. met	meet
2. thought	_____
3. had	_____
4. cut	_____
5. felt	_____
6. went	_____
7. began	_____

DISCUSSION AND WRITING

Discuss or write answers to these questions.

1. Discuss a time when two people gave you very different advice. Who did you listen to? Why? Was he or she right?

2. Pretend that the farmer is telling the story. Retell the story starting with the sentence, *One day, my son and I were on our way to the nearby market town to sell our donkey.*

JUST FOR FUN

1. Rewrite paragraphs 6, 7, and 8 of the story. Make up your own ending. Read and compare stories with your classmates.

2. Act out the story as a class or in groups.

Chapter 9

The Magic Box

a traditional folktale

BEFORE YOU READ A and B

1. People often tell stories about what happens when city people are in the country and country people are in the city. Why do you think these stories are popular? Do you know any stories like this?

2. Look at picture 1. Who and what do you see in that picture?

WHILE YOU READ

1. Read to the end of paragraph 2. Try to guess how the story ends.

2. The "magic box" is something you see in a lot of department stores and office buildings. As you read the story, try to guess what the magic box is.

■ ■ ■

The Magic Box

1   A plain country woman was visiting the city for the first time. She went into a very tall building. On the first floor, she saw an old lady standing in front of a door. The door was closed, and over the door, there were lights.

2   Then the door opened. The old lady standing in front of the door went inside. Then it closed. A few minutes later, the door opened again, and a beautiful young woman walked out! The country woman thought, "This is the door to a magic box! If I go inside the box, I will be beautiful when I come out."

3   She waited for the door to open again. Then she walked in. But inside the door, she saw a lot of buttons on the wall. And she didn't know what buttons to push!

COMPREHENSION

1 *Write* **T** *next to the sentences that are* **true**. *Write* **F** *next to the sentences that are* **false**.

1. _____ The box was really a magic box.

2. _____ The plain woman came from another country.

3. _____ The country woman became young and beautiful.

4. _____ The old lady became young and beautiful.

5. _____ The country woman entered the magic box.

2 *Number the sentences to show the correct story order.*

_____ The country woman went into a tall building.

_____ A beautiful young woman walked out of the magic box.

_____ An old lady walked into the magic box.

_____ The country woman saw many buttons on the wall.

_____ The country woman walked into the magic box.

VOCABULARY

Look back at the story. Find the sentence in the paragraph shown in the parentheses. Then, find the words that mean the same as the underlined words.

1. An <u>unattractive</u> country woman was visiting the city . . . (paragraph 1)

    unattractive _____

2. She went into a <u>skyscraper</u>. (paragraph 1)

    skyscraper _____

3. . . . she saw an <u>elderly</u> lady standing in front of a door. (paragraph 1)

    elderly _____

4. The door was <u>shut</u>, and over the door, there were lights. (paragraph 1)

    shut _____

GRAMMAR

Sometimes the subject is not at the beginning of the sentence. Underline the subject in the following sentences. Some sentences may have more than one clause, which means they will have more than one subject. The first one is done for you.

1. But inside the door, <u>she</u> saw a lot of buttons on the wall.

2. A few minutes later, the door opened again.

3. Over the door, there were lights.

4. On the first floor, she saw an old lady standing in front of a door.

5. "If I go inside the box, I will be beautiful when I come out."

WHILE YOU READ

1. Read to the end of paragraph 2. Try to guess how the story ends.

2. The "magic box" is something you see in a lot of department stores and office buildings. As you read the story, try to guess what the magic box is.

■ ■ ■

The Magic Box

1   An unattractive country woman who was visiting the city for the first time entered a skyscraper. On the ground floor, she noticed an old lady standing in front of a door. Over the door there were several lights.

2   As the country woman watched, the door opened and the elderly woman stepped inside. Then a few minutes later, the door opened again, and out came a beautiful young woman! The country woman was amazed. "This must be the door to a magic box!" she thought. "If I go inside, maybe I, too, will be beautiful when I come out!"

3   She waited for the door to open again. When it did, she eagerly walked in. Then she looked all around. She could see nothing but buttons on the wall, and she had no idea which one to push!

COMPREHENSION

Answer the following questions in pairs or small groups.

1. You see this "magic box" all the time. You may have one in your school.

   a. What is the "magic box"?
   b. What are the lights over the door?
   c. What are the buttons inside the magic box?
   d. Why didn't the country woman know what it was?

2. Think about the adjectives used in this story.

   a. Why is it important to know that the woman is unattractive?
   b. Why is it important to know that the woman is a country woman?
   c. Why is it important to know that the woman was visiting the city for the first time?

3. *. . . she had no idea which one to push!* What does this phrase mean?

    a. She didn't have any ideas.

    b. She wanted to push some buttons.

    c. She didn't know which button to push.

    d. She pushed all the buttons.

4. *She could see nothing but buttons . . .* What does this phrase mean?

    a. She saw nothing.

    b. She only saw buttons.

    c. She saw buttons and other things.

    d. She couldn't see.

5. Did the country woman become beautiful when she entered the magic box? Why or why not?

VOCABULARY

Match the words in the first column with their definitions in the second column.

1. ____ unattractive	**a.** the street level
2. ____ entered	**b.** saw
3. ____ a skyscraper	**c.** went into
4. ____ the ground floor	**d.** some
5. ____ noticed	**e.** ugly
6. ____ several	**f.** with great interest
7. ____ elderly	**g.** surprised
8. ____ amazed	**h.** didn't know
9. ____ eagerly	**i.** a very tall building
10. ____ nothing but	**j.** only
11. ____ had no idea	**k.** old

DICTIONARY SKILLS

Use your dictionary to find the definition and part of speech for each underlined word as it is used in the sentence.

1. In the United States, there are many farms in the <u>country</u> but few in the city or suburbs.

   definition _____

   part of speech _____

2. It is very difficult to move from one <u>country</u> to another.

   definition _____

   part of speech _____

3. Karen feels very <u>plain</u> because her sister is beautiful and Karen is not.

   definition _____

   part of speech _____

4. Some people like chocolate syrup on their ice cream but, I like to eat mine <u>plain</u>.

   definition _____

   part of speech _____

5. Some people live in the mountains; others live on the <u>plains</u>.

   definition _____

   part of speech _____

6. Put your toys back in the <u>box</u>.

   definition _____

   part of speech _____

7. Some people learn to <u>box</u> to protect themselves.

   definition _____

   part of speech _____

8. Helen waited for the door to <u>close</u>.

   definition _____

   part of speech _____

9. The car was so <u>close</u>, Mike was afraid it would hit him.

   definition _____

   part of speech _____

10. I am very <u>close</u> to my family.

definition _____

part of speech _____

GRAMMAR

Look back at the story. Find the sentence in the paragraph shown in parentheses. Then, answer the questions about the underlined words.

1. An unattractive country woman <u>who</u> was visiting the city for the first time <u>entered</u> a skyscraper. (paragraph 1)

   a. What does *who* refer to? _____

   b. What is the subject of *entered*? _____

2. When <u>it did,</u> <u>she</u> eagerly walked in. (paragraph 3)

   a. What is *it*? _____

   b. What did it *do*? _____

   c. Who is *she*? _____

3. <u>She</u> had no idea which <u>one</u> to push! (paragraph 3)

   a. Who was *she*? _____

   b. What does *one* refer to ?_____

DISCUSSION AND WRITING A and B

Discuss or write the answers to these questions.

1. What misunderstanding occurred in the story? Tell another ending to the story.

2. Tell a story about a city person being in the country or a country person being in the city.

3. If there really were a magic box that would make you more attractive, would you go into it? Why or why not?

JUST FOR FUN

1. Work in small groups to complete this puzzle.

Across
1. not pretty
6. opposite of *stop*
7. a special power to make things happen
10. opposite of *yes*
11. donate
12. together
13. opposite of *up*
15. entrance
18. old

Down
1. not pretty
2. opposite of *yes*
3. past of *think*
4. very surprised
5. anxiously
8. opposite of *out*
9. opposite of *city*
12. lady
14. opposite of *open*
15. opposite of *alive*
16. either
17. elderly

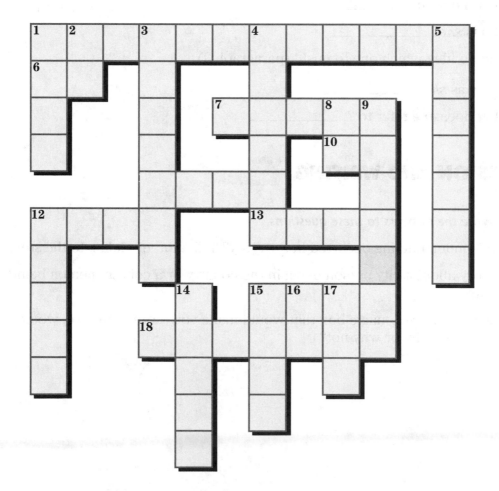

2. Find the following words in the puzzle. The words can be written across, up and down, forward, backward, or on an angle.

| plain | buttons | push | magic | box | country | city | lights |

```
s   t   h   g   i   l   y
n   p   u   s   a   r   t
d   u   l   x   s   q   i
x   s   m   a   g   i   c
o   h   d   o   i   o   r
b   u   t   t   o   n   s
c   o   u   n   t   r   y
```

Chapter 10

Juan Bobo and the Pot

a folktale from Puerto Rico

BEFORE YOU READ A and B

1. Look at the picture. Do you think this story takes place in the city or the country? Why?

2. Where is Juan Bobo sitting? Does he look happy or angry? How do you know?

Juan is a Spanish name similar to the English name *John*. It is pronounced *wan*.

WHILE YOU READ

1. In English, Juan Bobo's last name means "silly" or "foolish." There are many stories about Juan Bobo. In each story, he misunderstands some information or instruction. As you read, think about what Juan Bobo misunderstood this time.

2. Read to the end of paragraph 3. What do you think will happen next?

■ ■ ■

Juan Bobo and the Pot

1   One day, Juan Bobo's mother needed a very big pot. She wanted to make chicken and rice for many people. She said to Juan Bobo, "Go to my friend's house and ask for a big pot. Then come home quickly."

2   Juan Bobo went to the friend's house. She gave him a big pot. He started to carry the pot home. Then he put it down on the road and looked at it. It was very big and heavy. It was made of clay and it had three legs.

3   Then he said to the pot, "You have three legs and I have only two legs. You can carry me for a few minutes." Then Juan Bobo sat down inside the pot. But the pot did not move.

4   Juan Bobo got angry. He threw a stone at the clay pot and broke it. Then he carried the pieces of the broken pot home.

5   His mother was angry when she saw the broken pot. "You are stupid," she said. But Juan Bobo thought, "I am not a stupid person. Only a fool carries something with three legs."

COMPREHENSION

1 Write **T** next to the sentences that are **true**. Write **F** next to the sentences that are **false**.

1. _____ Juan's mother used the big pot to make dinner.

2. _____ Juan's mother thought Juan was stupid.

3. _____ The friend gave Juan a wood pot.

4. _____ The pot carried Juan home.

5. _____ The pot had three legs.

Answer the following questions in pairs or small groups.

1. What did Juan Bobo's mother want to cook?

2. Why did Juan Bobo's mother need a big pot?

3. What was the pot made of?

4. Why did Juan Bobo think the pot should carry him?

5. What happened to the pot?

6. How did Juan Bobo's mother feel when he came home?

VOCABULARY

Match the words in the first column with the words that mean the opposite in the second column.

1. ____ a friend	**a.** smart
2. ____ quickly	**b.** outside
3. ____ heavy	**c.** light
4. ____ inside	**d.** slowly
5. ____ broke	**e.** fixed
6. ____ stupid	**f.** nothing
7. ____ something	**g.** an enemy

GRAMMAR

Complete the sentences with the correct verb form.

carried	carries	carrying	carry

1. Juan didn't want to _____ the pot.

2. After _____ the pot for awhile, he put it down.

3. He _____ the broken pieces to his mother.

4. Only a stupid person _____ something with three legs.

| break | breaking | breaks | broke | broken |

5. Be careful not to _____ the pot.

6. He picked up the _____ pieces.

7. The fight with her boyfriend is _____ her heart.

8. Glass _____ easily, so be careful.

9. Who _____ the dish that was on the table?

B **WHILE YOU READ**

1. In English, Juan Bobo's last name means "silly" or "foolish." There are many stories about Juan Bobo. In each story, he misunderstands some information or instruction. As you read, think about what Juan Bobo misunderstood this time.

2. Read to the end of paragraph 3. What do you think will happen next?

■ ■ ■

Juan Bobo and the Pot

1   One day, Juan Bobo's mother wanted a very large pot. She needed it to make chicken and rice because she was expecting many guests for dinner. She asked Juan Bobo to hurry to a friend's house to borrow a big pot.

2   The friend lent him a large clay pot with three legs. Juan Bobo started to carry it home, but it was very big and heavy.

3   Soon he put the pot down on the road and said to it, "Why don't you carry me for awhile, since you have three legs and I have only two?" Of course, the pot said nothing. Then Juan Bobo climbed into the pot, but it didn't move.

4   Finally Juan Bobo got mad. He threw a rock at the pot and smashed it. Then he carried the broken pieces home. When his mother saw the broken pieces of the pot, she got angry and told him he was stupid.

5   Juan Bobo wondered why his mother thought he was stupid. He thought to himself, "I'm not stupid. A real fool is one who will carry something that has three legs."

COMPREHENSION

Number the sentences to show the correct order.

_____ Juan's mother was very angry.

_____ The friend gave Juan a big pot.

_____ Juan's mother asked him to get a pot from a friend.

_____ Juan sat in the pot.

_____ Juan started to carry the pot.

_____ Juan threw a rock at the pot.

VOCABULARY

1 *Match the words in the first column with their definitions in the second column.*

1. _____ large **a.** broke into many parts

2. _____ a pot **b.** small parts, bits

3. _____ expecting **c.** a stupid person

4. _____ guests **d.** people who are visiting someone's home

5. _____ to hurry **e.** a round, deep pan

6. _____ clay **f.** big

7. _____ to carry **g.** planning to have

8. _____ smashed **h.** to take something somewhere

9. _____ pieces **i.** wanted to know

10. _____ wondered **j.** to go quickly

11. _____ a fool **k.** heavy earth used to make dishes

2 *Circle the word in each row that means the opposite of the others.*

1. hurry   rush   go slowly   go quickly   speed

2. large   big   huge   small   gigantic

3. smash   fix   break   shatter   destroy

4. stupid   foolish   dumb   smart   idiotic

5. hold   throw   toss   hurl   fling

6. angry   mad   irate   annoyed   happy

Answer the following questions by looking back at the suggested paragraphs. The first one is done for you.

1. What word in paragraph 1 means the same as *big?*

   _____large_____

2. What word in paragraph 2 means the opposite of *borrowed?*

   _____

3. What word in paragraph 2 means the opposite of *light?*

   _____

4. What word in paragraph 4 means the same as *mad?*

   _____

DICTIONARY SKILLS

Use your dictionary to find the definition and the part of speech for each underlined word as it is used in the sentence.

1. Mary used a big <u>pot</u> for cooking stew.

   definition _____

   part of speech _____

2. The card players put money in the <u>pot</u> to start the game.

   definition _____

   part of speech _____

3. I <u>wonder</u> if I passed the test.

   definition _____

   part of speech _____

4. Niagara Falls is one of the natural <u>wonders</u> of the world.

   definition _____

   part of speech _____

5. This <u>leg</u> of my trip takes me to Europe.

   definition _____

   part of speech _____

6. The pot had three <u>legs</u>.

definition _____

part of speech _____

7. Mark threw a <u>rock</u> and broke a window.

definition _____

part of speech _____

8. The boat <u>rocked</u> dangerously in the high waves.

definition _____

part of speech _____

9. I like <u>rock</u> music if it isn't too loud.

definition _____

part of speech _____

10. Juan's mother was <u>expecting</u> guests for dinner.

definition _____

part of speech _____

11. Karen must eat properly and rest because she is <u>expecting</u> a baby.

definition _____

part of speech _____

GRAMMAR

1 *Look back at the story. Find the sentence in the paragraph shown in parentheses. Then, write who or what the underlined word refers to.*

1. <u>She</u> asked Juan Bobo to hurry to a friend's house . . . (paragraph 1)

she _____

2. . . . <u>it</u> was very big and heavy. (paragraph 2)

it _____

3. . . . I have only <u>two</u>. (paragraph 3)

two _____

4. <u>He</u> threw a rock at the pot and smashed <u>it</u>. (paragraph 4)

he _____ it _____

2 *Some of these verbs from the story are regular and some are irregular. Write the simple past tense form of these verbs. Use your dictionary if you need help.*

Base	Past
1. want	_____
2. need	_____
3. is	_____
4. ask	_____
5. borrow	_____
6. lend	_____
7. carry	_____
8. throw	_____
9. get	_____
10. see	_____
11. tell	_____
12. think	_____
13. put	_____
14. wonder	_____

DISCUSSION AND WRITING

Discuss or write answers to these questions.

1. Do you know a person like Juan Bobo? Tell something funny or silly that person did.

2. Tell a story that you have read about a character who always does foolish things.

3. Discuss a foolish thing that you once did that made your parents angry.

Read the Juan Bobo story below and guess the end.

Juan Bobo Carries Water

Juan Bobo's mother called him and handed him two empty buckets. She said, "I want you to fill these buckets for me with water from the stream." But Juan Bobo replied that the buckets would be too heavy to carry if they were full of water. His mother said, "Then use something else, but bring me some water!"

Juan Bobo returned a little later. "Mama, I brought you the water. And I think I am getting stronger! As I walked back from the stream, the water felt lighter and lighter!"

Write your own ending to the story that explains why the water felt lighter as he walked back from the stream and what he used to carry the water. Then, look below to see how the story ends.

Just then, Juan's mother stepped in a puddle. "Juan! Is this the water you brought me from the stream?"

"No, Mama, the water I brought you is in these two baskets."

Chapter 11

The Wolf and the Stork

a traditional folktale

BEFORE YOU READ

1. Look at the pictures. Which animal is the wolf? Which animal is the stork? Describe them.

2. What problem does the stork have in picture 1?

3. What problem does the wolf have in picture 2?

A WHILE YOU READ

1. Read to the end of paragraph 3. What do you think the stork will do?

2. There is a saying "He who laughs last laughs best." What do you think it means? As you read, think about how that saying fits the story. Which animal laughs last?

The Wolf and the Stork

1   A long, long time ago, the wolf and the stork were friends. One day, the wolf asked the stork to come to his house to eat.

2   When the stork arrived at the wolf's house, the wolf put two bowls of soup on the table. The wolf ate his bowl of soup quickly. When he finished, he asked the stork, "Did you like my soup?"

3   But the stork was angry because he couldn't eat the soup. His beak was too long! When the stork went home, he was still hungry. The wolf laughed and laughed.

4   Then the stork had an idea. He asked the wolf to come to dinner. He filled two tall pitchers with good soup. They began to eat. When the stork finished eating, he asked the wolf if he wanted more to eat.

5   But the wolf was angry. His mouth was so big that he couldn't get it into the pitcher. The wolf went home hungry, and the stork laughed and laughed.

Moral: He who laughs last laughs best.

COMPREHENSION

1 *Write **T** next to the sentences that are **true** and **F** next to the sentences that are **false**. Write **X** if you do not have enough information to tell if the sentence is true or false.*

1. _____ The stork couldn't eat from a pitcher.

2. _____ The stork had trouble eating soup from a bowl.

3. _____ The wolf was sorry that his friend couldn't eat the soup.

4. _____ The wolf ate a good meal at the stork's house.

5. _____ The wolf finished the first bowl of soup quickly.

2 *Complete the paragraphs with the correct words from the story. The first one is done for you.*

A long, long time ago the ___wolf___ and the stork were friends. One day, the wolf asked the _____ to come to his house to eat.

When the stork _____ at the wolf's _____ , the wolf put two _____ of soup on the table. The wolf ate his bowl of soup _____ . When he finished, he _____ the stork, "Did you like my _____ ?"

But the stork was _____ because he couldn't eat the soup. His _____ was too long! When the stork went home, he was still _____ . The wolf laughed and _____

Then the stork had an _____ . He asked the _____ to come to dinner. He filled two tall _____ with good soup. They began to eat. When the stork finished _____ , he asked the _____ if he wanted more to eat.

But the wolf was angry. His _____ was so big that he couldn't get it into the pitcher. The _____ went home hungry, and the _____ laughed and laughed.

VOCABULARY

Match the words in the first column with their definitions in the second column.

1. _____ a stork   **a.** a thought or plan

2. _____ a bowl   **b.** a deep rounded dish or container

3. _____ angry   **c.** the mouth of a bird

4. _____ a beak   **d.** a tall, white bird with long legs

5. _____ an idea   **e.** a tall container for liquids

6. _____ filled   **f.** made full

7. _____ a pitcher   **g.** unhappy, upset

GRAMMAR

Write the base form of these simple past tense verbs from the story.

Past	Base		Past	Base
1. were	_____		6. was	_____
2. arrived	_____		7. went	_____
3. ate	_____		8. laughed	_____
4. asked	_____		9. filled	_____
5. did	_____		10. began	_____

WHILE YOU ARE READING

1. Read to the end of paragraph 3. What do you think the stork will do?

2. There is a saying "He who laughs last laughs best." What do you think it means? As you read, think about how that saying fits the story. Which animal laughs last?

The Wolf and the Stork

1   Long ago, a stork and a wolf lived in the countryside. One day, the wolf invited his friend the stork to dine at his house. The stork happily agreed to come.

2   When they sat down to eat, the wolf put two bowls of soup on the table. The soup smelled delicious! When the wolf finished eating his soup, he asked the stork how it tasted.

3   But the stork was angry because he couldn't eat the soup with his long beak. When the stork went home hungry, the wolf laughed and laughed.

4   Then the stork decided to get even with the wolf. He invited the wolf to his home for dinner. When the wolf came, the stork filled two pitchers with delicious soup. They began to eat. As soon as the stork finished eating, he offered the wolf a second helping.

5   But the wolf was angry because his big snout wouldn't fit in the pitcher. The wolf went home with an empty stomach, and the stork just laughed and laughed.

Moral: He who laughs last laughs best.

COMPREHENSION

Answer the following questions in pairs or small groups.

1. What food did the wolf serve?

2. Why couldn't the stork eat at the wolf's house?

3. Why couldn't the wolf eat at the stork's house?

4. Do you think the wolf and the stork are still friends? Why or why not?

VOCABULARY

Circle the correct meaning of the following phrases.

1. *Get even* means
   a. have more than.
   b. get something new.
   c. get back at.
   d. be angry at.

2. *As soon as* means
   a. at the same time as.
   b. right before.
   c. right after.
   d. when possible.

3. *Second helping* means
   a. more help or assistance.
   b. more food.
   c. two friends.
   d. being hungry.

4. *Have an empty stomach* means
   a. be hungry.
   b. be full.
   c. be angry.
   d. have stomach pains.

DICTIONARY SKILLS

Use your dictionary to find the definition and part of speech for each underlined word as it is used in the sentence.

1. Stacy filled the <u>pitcher</u> with iced tea.

   definition _____

   part of speech _____

2. Melanie was the <u>pitcher</u> on her softball team.

   definition _____

   part of speech _____

3. Robert likes to <u>bowl</u> with his friends.

   definition _____

   part of speech _____

4. Jodie filled the dog's <u>bowl</u> with water.

   definition _____

   part of speech _____

5. Ian exercises regularly because he wants to stay physically <u>fit</u>.

   definition _____

   part of speech _____

6. That shirt doesn't <u>fit</u> me.

   definition _____

   part of speech _____

7. Shari has good <u>taste</u>; her clothes always look nice.

   definition _____

   part of speech _____

8. These cookies <u>taste</u> delicious.

   definition _____

   part of speech _____

9. I'd like a second <u>helping</u> of meat.

definition _____

part of speech _____

10. Mary is <u>helping</u> her mother in the garden.

definition _____

part of speech _____

GRAMMAR

1 *Combine each pair of sentences using the words in parentheses. Remember that the words in parentheses sometimes go at the beginning of the sentence.*

1. The wolf finished his soup. He asked the stork how it tasted.

(when) _____

2. The stork was angry. He couldn't eat the soup with his long beak.

(because) _____

3. The stork finished. He offered the wolf a second helping.

(as soon as) _____

2 *Some verbs can be followed by the* **to** *(infinitive) form of a verb. Some can be followed by the* **-ing** *(gerund) form of a verb. Some verbs can be followed by either. Sometimes there is no change in meaning; sometimes there is.*

Finish is followed by a gerund (*-ing* form).

Example: finish talking   finish shopping

Start can be followed by the gerund or the infinitive without any difference in meaning.

Example: Start talking. <u>or</u> Start to talk.

Stop followed by a gerund means "don't do" (something).

Example: Stop talking to your friend. (Don't talk to your friend.)

Stop followed by an infinitive (*to* form) means "in order to do" (something).

Example: Stop to talk to your friend. (Stop whatever else you are doing in order to talk to your friend.)

*Complete the sentences using the infinitive (**to**) or gerund (-**ing**) form of the verb in parentheses. The first one is done for you.*

1. (eat)   The wolf finished ____eating____ the soup.

2. (laugh)   The stork started _____ because the wolf couldn't eat the food.

3. (study)   The students stopped _____ and watched television instead.

4. (watch)   The students began walking home, but they stopped _____ the soccer game in the schoolyard.

5. (dine)   They usually finish _____ at 7:00.

6. (pop)   Children, please stop _____ the balloons; I need them for the party.

DISCUSSION AND WRITING

Discuss or write the answers to these questions.

1. Discuss the following sayings and explain how they fit this story.

   • "Don't get mad. Get even." In this story, who got even?

   • "Revenge is sweet." What is revenge? Who got revenge in this story?

2. What do you know about the wolf and stork? Would you like them to be your friends? Why or why not?

3. Did you ever play a trick on a friend, or did anyone ever play a trick on you? How did you feel about it? Explain what happened.

JUST FOR FUN

Working in pairs, rewrite this story in the form of a dialogue. Then act out your dialogue for the class.

Example: WOLF: Come to my house for dinner.

              STORK: Thank you. I will.

Chapter 12

The Tortoise and the Hare

a traditional folktale

BEFORE YOU READ A and B

1. Look at the pictures. Which animal is the tortoise? Do you know another name for *tortoise*?

2. Which animal is the hare? Do you know another name for *hare*?

3. What do you know about tortoises and hares?

WHILE YOU READ

1. As you read, find three things the tortoise (turtle) did to affect who won the race.

2. As you read, find three things the hare (rabbit) did to affect who won the race.

■ ■ ■

The Tortoise and the Hare

1   A long, long time ago, a rabbit and a turtle wanted to have a race. The rabbit was very fast. The turtle was very slow.

2   The night before the race, the turtle went to sleep early. On the morning of the race, he got up early. He started running at 8:00.

3   The rabbit didn't worry about the race. He knew that he was faster than the turtle. The night before the race, he stayed up late at a party. He woke up late for the race. The race started at 8:00, but he didn't start running until 9:00.

4   Because the rabbit was so fast, he quickly passed the turtle. When he was far ahead, he stopped to talk with some friends. He was very busy talking. He didn't see the turtle run past him.

5   The turtle ran and ran. But the rabbit raced past him again. Soon the rabbit was far ahead of the turtle. He thought that he had a lot of time, so he stopped to eat a big lunch. After the rabbit ate, he had to run slowly. He felt very tired from all the food, so he stopped to rest. Soon he fell asleep. While he was sleeping, the turtle passed him again.

6   When the rabbit woke up, he ran very fast. But it was too late. The turtle had won the race.

COMPREHENSION

1 *Write **T** next to the sentences that are **true**. Write **F** next to the sentences that are **false**.*

1. _____ The rabbit could run faster than the turtle.

2. _____ The rabbit didn't start the race on time.

3. _____ The turtle stopped to have lunch.

4. _____ The rabbit stopped to talk to some friends.

5. ____ The rabbit was faster, so he won the race.

6. ____ The rabbit couldn't run fast after he ate.

7. ____ The rabbit slept soon after he ate.

8. ____ The rabbit went to a party the night before the race.

9. ____ The turtle went to sleep late the night before the race.

10. ____ The rabbit started running at 8:00.

2 *Number the sentences to show the correct story order.*

____ The rabbit woke up.

____ The turtle started running in the race.

____ The rabbit ate a big lunch.

____ The rabbit started running in the race.

____ The rabbit went to a party.

____ The turtle won the race.

____ The rabbit stopped to talk to his friends.

____ The rabbit and the turtle wanted to have a race.

3 *Answer the following questions in pairs or in small groups.*

1. Which animal was faster?

2. Which animal prepared for the race? How?

3. What time did the race begin?

4. Why was the rabbit late for the start of the race?

5. Which animal won the race?

VOCABULARY

Look back at the story. Find the sentence in the paragraph shown in parentheses. Then find the words that mean the same as the underlined words.

1. Because the <u>hare</u> was so <u>quick</u>, he quickly <u>overtook</u> the <u>tortoise</u>. (paragraph 4)

hare _____   overtook _____

quick _____   tortoise _____

2. When he was far <u>out in front</u>, he <u>paused</u> to <u>chat</u> with some <u>buddies</u>. (paragraph 4)

out in front _____   chat _____

paused _____   buddies _____

3. He felt <u>exhausted</u> from all the food, so he stopped to <u>take a nap</u>. (paragraph 5)

exhausted _____   take a nap _____

GRAMMAR

Combine each pair of sentences using the words in parentheses. The first one is done for you.

1. The rabbit had a lot of time. He stopped to eat a big lunch.

(so) The rabbit had a lot of time, so he stopped to eat a big lunch.

2. The rabbit was very fast. The turtle was very slow.

(but) _____

3. He felt tired from all the food. He stopped to rest.

(so) _____

4. The race started at 8:00. He didn't start running until 9:00.

(but) _____

PRONUNCIATION AND SPELLING

Homophones *are words that sound the same but have different spellings, such as* **here** *and* **hear**. *Complete the sentences with homophones from the list.*

passed / past   hare / hair   won / one   knew / new

1. The rabbit _____ that he was faster than the turtle.

2. The rabbit quickly _____ the turtle.

3. Lisa has beautiful brown _____ .

4. Another word for *rabbit* is _____ .

5. While the rabbit was sleeping, the turtle ran _____ him.

6. Because he never stopped running, the turtle _____ the race.

7. I just bought a _____ car.

8. I like your car so much that I may buy _____ just like it.

WHILE YOU READ

1. As you read, find three things the tortoise did to affect who won the race

2. As you read, find three things the hare did to affect who won the race.

■ ■ ■

The Tortoise and the Hare

1   Once upon a time, a tortoise and a hare decided to have a race. The hare was a very fast runner, but the tortoise was very slow.

2   To prepare for the race, the tortoise went to sleep early. On the morning of the race, he woke up promptly so that he could be at the starting line at 8:00.

3   The hare didn't prepare for the race because he knew that he was faster than the tortoise. The hare stayed up late at a party. On the morning of the race, he overslept. Although he was supposed to start running at 8:00, he didn't begin until 9:00.

4   Because the hare was so quick, he soon overtook the tortoise. When the hare was out in front, he paused to chat with some friends. The hare was so busy talking that he didn't see the tortoise pass him.

5   The tortoise went steadily on and on. He never stopped or rested. But the hare raced past him again and was soon very far ahead. The hare was hungry, so he stopped to have a big meal. When he was full, he couldn't run very fast. All the food made him feel so sleepy that he stopped to take a nap.

6   While the hare was sleeping, the tortoise passed him again. When the hare awoke, he raced as fast as he could. But he was too late! The tortoise had already crossed the finish line.

COMPREHENSION

Answer the following questions in pairs or small groups.

1. Why didn't the hare go to sleep early the night before the race?

2. Why did the hare take a nap?

3. The hare was much faster than the tortoise, but the tortoise was ahead at the beginning, the middle, and the end of the race. How did the tortoise get ahead each time?

4. What time did the tortoise start running?

5. What time did the hare start running?

VOCABULARY

1 *Match the words in the first column with their definitions in the second column.*

1. _____ a hare   **a.** completed the race

2. _____ to prepare   **b.** food eaten at one time

3. _____ promptly   **c.** fast

4. _____ overslept   **d.** to get ready

5. _____ quick   **e.** in front

6. _____ overtook   **f.** on time

7. _____ paused   **g.** went ahead of someone

8. _____ to chat   **h.** a kind of rabbit

9. _____ steadily   **i.** stopped for a short time

10. _____ ahead   **j.** to talk in a friendly way

11. _____ a meal   **k.** at an even speed

12. _____ crossed the finish line   **l.** woke up late

2 *Three of the words or phrases in each of these rows have almost the same meaning. Circle the word or phrase that has a different meaning.*

1. swift   slow   fast   quick

2. prompt   on time   late   timely

3. overtake   pass   run past   fall behind

4. wake up   take a nap   rest   sleep

5. out in front   in the rear   ahead   in the lead

3 *Write the words that describe the hare in the **Rabbit** column. Write the words that describe the tortoise in the **Turtle** column. Use a dictionary if you need help.*

prompt	late	overconfident	fast
persistent	slow	irresponsible	reliable
consistent	steady	sleepy	lazy

Rabbit   **Turtle**

_____   _____
_____   _____
_____   _____
_____   _____
_____   _____
_____   _____

GRAMMAR

*Complete the sentences using the gerund (**-ing**) form or infinitive (**to**) form of the verbs in parentheses. (Hint: Remember that **stop** can be followed by -**ing** or **to**, but the meaning is different.)*

Example: I stopped to sing. (I stopped what I was doing so that I could sing.)

Example: I stopped singing. (I am no longer singing.)

1. The tortoise never stopped (run) _____, but the hare stopped (chat) _____ with his friends.

2. The tortoise wanted (prepare) _____ for the race, so he went (sleep) _____ early.

3. The hare was hungry, so he stopped (have) _____ a big meal.

4. The food made the hare sleepy, so he stopped (take) _____ a nap.

5. The tortoise never stopped (rest) _____ .

DISCUSSION AND WRITING

Discuss or write answers to these questions.

1. How is the tortoise in this story like the ants in "The Ant and the Cicada"? How is the hare similar to the cicadas?

2. There is a saying "Slow but steady wins the race." How does that saying describe what happened in this story?

3. Are you more like the tortoise or the hare? Explain.

4. Do you know a person like the tortoise? Do you know a person like the hare? Which one would you rather work with? Why? Which one would you rather go to a party with? Why?

JUST FOR FUN A and B

1. In groups of three or four, act out one of the stories in this book that the class has already read. Do this without using words. The rest of the class will guess which story you are presenting.

2. Play the game Twenty Questions. Individually or in a group, choose a person or an object from one of the stories the class has already read. The rest of the class may ask you up to twenty questions to find out who or what you chose. The questions have to be answered *yes* or *no*.

Chapter 13

A THIEF'S STORY

a traditional folktale

BEFORE YOU READ A and B

1. What is a thief? Why do you think people become thieves?

2. What happens to thieves who are caught?

3. How do children learn the difference between right and wrong? Who are a child's first teachers?

4. Look at picture 1. The people look happy. Look at picture 3. The people look upset. Read the story to see what happened.

WHILE YOU READ

1. Read to the end of paragraph 2. What do you think the boy will ask for?

2. Read to the end of paragraph 3. What reason will the boy give for his action?

■ ■ ■

A THIEF'S STORY

1   Once upon a time, there was a poor family. They had one son. The son often went out to steal things. Every time he brought something home, his mother was happy. She didn't ask him how and where he got it. She just said, "That's very good."

2   Many years passed. The little boy grew up and became a full-time thief. One day the police caught him and took him to jail. In court, the judge said that he must die for his crimes. But before dying, he could have one last wish.

3   The son asked for his mother. He said that he wanted to see her tongue. The mother came and stuck out her tongue. Then the son cut his mother's tongue until it was bleeding. Everyone was surprised. They wanted to know why he hurt his mother.

4   The son answered, "My mother did not tell me it was wrong to steal. And so I am here now."

5   The judge decided that the son should not die. Later the judge let the son go free. The son became an honest man and lived to an old age.

COMPREHENSION

1 *Write* **T** *next to the sentences that are* **true** *and* **F** *next to the sentences that are* **false.**
Write **X** *if the story doesn't give this information.*

1. _____ The son cut his mother's tongue.

2. _____ The mother didn't want her son to steal.

3. _____ The son died because he was a thief.

4. _____ The police took the son to jail.

5. _____ The son was angry at his mother.

6. _____ The mother was a thief.

7. ____ The judge decided that the son should not die.

8. ____ The thief became an honest man.

9. ____ The thief was young when he died.

10. ____ The son and his mother lived in a small house.

2 *Number the sentences to show the correct order.*

____ The police took the son to jail.

____ The mother said, "That's very good."

____ The son became an honest man.

____ The son cut his mother's tongue.

____ The judge said he must die.

____ The son became a full-time thief.

____ The mother stuck out her tongue.

____ The son was given one last wish.

3 *Answer the following questions in pairs or small groups.*

1. How did this story begin? What are some other story openers?

2. How did the boy get the things that he brought to his mother?

3. How did the mother act when her son stole things for her?

4. Why did the thief cut his mother's tongue?

5. Many stories end with the sentence *He lived happily ever after.* What ending is used in this story?

VOCABULARY

Match the words in the first column with their definitions in the second column.

1. ____ to steal   **a.** losing blood

2. ____ a court   **b.** the person in control of a court

3. ____ a judge   **c.** acts that are wrong and can be punished by the law

4. ____ crimes   **d.** put out, pushed out

5. ____ stuck out   **e.** the place where decisions about the law are made

6. ____ bleeding   **f.** to take something that belongs to someone else

7. ____ honest   **g.** truthful and sincere

GRAMMAR

1 *Write the simple past tense form of these irregular verbs. Use your dictionary if you need help.*

Base	Past	Base	Past
1. go	_____	6. steal	_____
2. stick	_____	7. become	_____
3. come	_____	8. bleed	_____
4. tell	_____	9. take	_____
5. cut	_____	10. catch	_____

2 In sentences that begin with *There is* or *There are*, the subject comes after the verb and the verb agrees with the subject.

Example: There was a poor man.

Subject: man   **Verb:** was

Example: There are many books on the table.

Subject: books   **Verb:** are

Complete the sentences with **is** *or* **are**. *Then circle the subject. The first one is done for you.*

1. There _____is_____ full (moon) tonight.

2. There _____ also many stars in the sky.

3. There _____ many thieves in jail.

4. There _____ several stories in this book.

5. There _____ a moral to this story.

SPELLING AND PRONUNCIATION

1 *Some words ending in* **-f** *form their plural by changing the* **f** *to* **v** *and adding* **-es**. *Write the plural for these words. The first one is done for you.*

Singular	Plural	Singular	Plural
1. thief	thieves	4. wife	_____
2. knife	_____	5. wolf	_____
3. life	_____	6. leaf	_____

WHILE YOU READ

1. Read to the end of paragraph 2. What do you think the boy will ask for?

2. Read to the end of paragraph 3. What reason will the boy give for his action?

■ ■ ■

A THIEF'S STORY

1   Once upon a time, there was a poor family who had one son. He used to go out and steal things. Whatever he brought home, his mother accepted. Once he brought back some eggs. Instead of asking him how and where he got them, she just praised him and said, "Well done!"

2   As the years passed, the little boy grew up to become a professional thief. The police arrested him and took him to prison. When he went to court, the judge sentenced him to death for his crimes. But before dying, he was given one last request.

3   He asked the prison guard to bring his mother to him so that he could see her tongue. When the mother came, she stuck her tongue out. The son reached over and cut it until it bled! Everyone was astonished and wondered why he had done such a thing.

4   The son explained, "Instead of warning me not to steal, my mother praised me. If she had told me it was wrong to take things that belong to someone else, I would not be here now."

5   Later the judge gave him a pardon. He became an honest man and lived to a ripe old age.

COMPREHENSION

Answer the following questions in pairs or small groups.

1. How do we know that the thief's mother approved of his stealing?

2. Why did the thief go to court?

3. What sentence did the thief receive?

4. In paragraph 3 it says, *Everyone was astonished and wondered why he had done such a thing.* What did he do? Why did he do it? Was he right or wrong to do it?

5. What happened to the thief in the end?

VOCABULARY

1 *Match the words in the first column with their definitions in the second column.*

1. _____ brought   **a.** told the reason

2. _____ accepted   **b.** surprised

3. _____ instead   **c.** caught by police for doing something wrong

4. _____ praised   **d.** took what was offered

5. _____ arrested   **e.** expressed approval

6. _____ astonished   **f.** an official order to forgive a crime

7. _____ explained   **g.** to be owned by someone

8. _____ to belong to   **h.** in place of

9. _____ a pardon   **i.** carried to

2 *Three of the words or phrases in each row have the same meaning. Circle the word or phrase that has a different meaning.*

1. thief	burglar	robber	judge
2. prison	home	jail	penitentiary
3. request	ask for	give	express desire for
4. evil	honest	trustworthy	truthful

3 *All of the following words relate to law or the legal system. Some were in the story; others were not. In pairs or small groups, discuss the meaning of these words.*

thief	arrest	police	prison	guard	court
trial	sentence	last request	pardon	jury	judge

Write two more words that relate to law.

_____

DICTIONARY SKILLS

Use your dictionary to find the definition and part of speech for each underlined word as it is used in the sentence.

1. Define the underlined word as it is used in this <u>sentence</u>.

   definition _____

   part of speech _____

2. Did the judge <u>sentence</u> him to five years in jail?

   definition _____

   part of speech _____

3. He cut his mother's <u>tongue</u>.

   definition _____

   part of speech _____

4. What is your native <u>tongue</u>?

   definition _____

   part of speech _____

GRAMMAR

Complete the sentences with the correct verb forms.

bled	bleed	bleeding	bleeds	blood

1. Marty's nose is _____ .

2. The patient has lost a lot of _____ .

3. When Tim cut his finger yesterday, it _____ .

4. Sometimes my nose _____ when I have a cold.

5. When people _____ too much, they feel tired.

steal	stealing	steals	stole	stolen

6. The police found the thief in the _____ car.

7. A person who _____ may go to jail.

8. This is the man who _____ your car yesterday.

9. It is wrong to _____

10. _____ is a serious crime.

DISCUSSION AND WRITING A and B

Discuss or write answers to these questions.

1. Many movies and television shows are about law. Tell a story that you saw in a movie or on television using as many of the words from Vocabulary Exercise 3 on page 112 as you can.

2. If you were on the jury in this story, would you have sentenced the thief to death? Why or why not?

3. If you were the judge, would you have pardoned the thief? Why or why not?

4. Is there a moral to this story? What is it?

5. Discuss the saying "As the twig is bent, so the tree inclines." What does the saying have to do with this story?

6. Discuss the saying "Honesty is the best policy." What does the saying have to do with this story?

JUST FOR FUN A and B

Go back to Vocabulary Exercise 3 on page 112. With a partner, write a short story using at least five of these words. Read your story to the class.

Chapter 14

The Story of the Smart Parrot

BEFORE YOU READ

1. Look at the picture. The bird in the picture is called a parrot. Parrots are talking birds that can repeat words or sounds that they hear. Have you ever heard a talking bird?

2. Do you think talking birds understand the words they hear or say? Why or why not?

3. The bird in this story is stubborn, which means that he is determined to do something others don't want him to do, or not do something others want him to do. Have you ever been stubborn? What happened as a result?

A WHILE YOU READ

1. Read to the end of paragraph 1. Do you think the bird will ever say what the man wants him to say?

2. Read to the end of paragraph 5. What do you think the man saw?

■ ■ ■

The Story of the Smart Parrot

1   A man in Puerto Rico had a wonderful parrot. There was no other parrot like him. He was very, very smart. This parrot would say any word—except one. He would not say the name of the town where he was born. The name of that town was Cataño.

2   The man tried and tried to teach the parrot to say *Cataño*. But the bird would not say the word. At first the man was very nice, but then he got angry. "You stupid bird! Why can't you say that word? Say *Cataño*, or I'll kill you!" But the parrot would not say it. Then the man got so angry that he shouted over and over, "Say *Cataño*, or I'll kill you!" But the bird wouldn't talk.

3   One day after trying for many hours to make the bird say *Cataño*, the man got very, very angry. He picked up the bird and threw him into the chicken house. "You are more stupid than the chickens. Soon I will eat them, and I will eat you, too."

4   In the chicken house there were four old chickens. They were for Sunday's dinner. The man put the parrot in the chicken house and left.

5   The next day the man came back to the chicken house. He opened the door and stopped. He was very surprised at what he saw!

6   He saw three dead chickens on the floor. The parrot was screaming at the fourth chicken, "Say *Cataño*, or I'll kill you!"

COMPREHENSION

1 *Write **T** next to the sentences that are **true**. Write **F** next to the sentences that are **false**.*

1. _____ The parrot could not say *Cataño*.

2. _____ The parrot would not say *Cataño* for the man.

3. _____ The chickens couldn't say *Cataño*.

4. _____ The parrot was more stupid than the chickens.

5. _____ The man ate the parrot for dinner.

6. _____ The man killed the chickens.

7. _____ The man got angry at the parrot.

8. _____ The parrot could say many words.

9. _____ The parrot killed the chickens.

10. _____ *Cataño* was the name of the parrot.

2 *Number the sentences to show the correct story order.*

_____ The man saw three dead chickens on the floor.

_____ The man tried to teach the parrot to say *Cataño*.

_____ The man threw the parrot into the chicken house.

_____ The parrot yelled, "Say *Cataño*, or I'll kill you."

_____ The man said, "Say *Cataño*, or I'll kill you."

VOCABULARY

Circle the word in each row that is different from the others.

1.	chicken	man	bird	parrot
2.	screaming	yelling	shouting	trying
3.	angry	wonderful	amazing	surprising
4.	tried	attempted	wanted	struggled
5.	flung	tossed	threw	caught

GRAMMAR

Combine each pair of sentences using the words in parentheses.

1. At first the man was very nice. He got angry.

   (but then) _____

2. The man got so angry that he shouted. The bird wouldn't talk.

   (but) _____

3. The man got very, very, angry. He picked up the bird and threw him into the chicken house.

   (so) _____

WHILE YOU READ

1. Read to the end of paragraph 1. Do you think the bird will ever say what the man wants him to say?

2. Read to the end of paragraph 5. What do you think the man saw?

The Story of the Smart Parrot

1   There was once a man in Puerto Rico who had a wonderful parrot. The parrot was unique; there was no other like him in the whole world. He could learn to say any word—except one. He would not say the name of his native town, Cataño.

2   The man did everything he could to teach the parrot to say *Cataño*, but he never succeeded. At first he was very gentle with the bird, but gradually he lost his temper. "You stupid bird! Why can't you learn to say that one word? Say *Cataño*, or I'll kill you!" But the parrot would not say it. Many times the man screamed, "Say *Cataño*, or I'll kill you!" But the bird would not repeat the name.

3   Finally the man gave up. He picked up the parrot and threw him into the chicken house. "You are even more stupid than the chickens."

4   In the chicken house there were four old chickens, waiting to be killed for Sunday's dinner.

5   The next morning, the man went out to the chicken house. When he opened the door, he was shocked by what he saw. He could not believe his eyes and ears!

6   On the floor lay three dead chickens. The parrot was screaming at the fourth, "Say *Cataño*, or I'll kill you!"

COMPREHENSION

Answer the following questions in pairs or small groups.

1. Why was the man angry at the parrot?

2. What did the man do to the parrot?

3. What did the man want to do with the chickens?

4. Why was the man surprised when he went to the chicken house?

5. How did the three chickens die?

6. *Cataño* was the name of the

    a. bird.

    b. man.

    c. town.

7. *He could not believe his eyes* means:

    a. He didn't like his eyes.

    b. He couldn't see.

    c. He saw something unbelievable.

VOCABULARY

1 *Match the words in the first column with their definitions in the second column.*

1. ____ unique	**a.** not including
2. ____ except	**b.** lifted
3. ____ native	**c.** yelled
4. ____ succeeded	**d.** the only one of its kind
5. ____ gentle	**e.** slowly, over a period of time
6. ____ gradually	**f.** to say or do something again
7. ____ lost his temper	**g.** very surprised
8. ____ screamed	**h.** did well; did what you tried to do
9. ____ to repeat	**i.** got very angry
10. ____ picked up	**j.** kind, calm
11. ____ shocked	**k.** relating to where you were born

2 *Circle the word in each row that is different from the others.*

1.	shocked	happy	amazed	astounded
2.	quickly	gradually	slowly	eventually
3.	lost his temper	got angry	got mad	was shocked
4.	murder	kill	claim	slay

3 *Look back at the paragraph shown in parentheses. Then, answer the questions about the underlined words.*

1. What phrase tells the meaning of <u>unique</u>? (paragraph 1)

   _____

2. What phrase means <u>the place where one is born</u>? (paragraph 1)

   _____

3. What phrase means <u>slowly got angry</u>? (paragraph 2)

   _____

4. What phrase explains the meaning of <u>shocked</u>? (paragraph 5)

   _____

DICTIONARY SKILLS

Use your dictionary to find the definition and part of speech for each underlined word as it is used in the sentence.

1. The man lost his <u>temper</u>.

   definition _____

   part of speech _____

2. In "A Thief's Story," the judge <u>tempered</u> justice with mercy.

   definition _____

   part of speech _____

3. The pole was made of <u>tempered</u> steel.

   definition _____

   part of speech _____

4. The man was <u>shocked</u> by what he saw.

   definition _____

   part of speech _____

5. The man was <u>shocked</u> when he touched the electric wire.

   definition _____

   part of speech _____

GRAMMAR

1 *Look back at the story. Find the sentence in the paragraph shown in parentheses. Then, answer the questions about the underlined words.*

1. . . . there was no <u>other</u> like him . . . (paragraph 1) No other what?

   _____

2. "Why can't you learn to say that <u>one word</u>?" (paragraph 2) What one word?

   _____

3. But the bird would not repeat <u>the name</u>. s(paragraph 2) What name?

   _____

4. . . . he was shocked by <u>what he saw</u>. (paragraph 5) What did he see?

   _____

5. The parrot was screaming at the <u>fourth</u> . . . (paragraph 6) The fourth what?

   _____

2 *Combine each pair of sentences using the words or instructions in parentheses.*

1. There was once a man in Puerto Rico. He had a wonderful parrot.

   (who) _____

2. The man opened the door. He was shocked by what he saw.

   (when) _____

3. There were four old chickens. They were waiting to be killed for Sunday's dinner.

   (Reduce the second sentence to an *-ing* phrase.)

   _____

4. The man had a parrot. The parrot was unique. (Use only the word *unique*

   from the second sentence.)

   _____

DISCUSSION AND WRITING

Discuss or write answers to these questions.

1. *Character* means "all the qualities that make a person, place, or thing different from another." What do you know about the character of the man?

2. What do you know about the character of the parrot?

3. Do you know any other story about a bird? Tell it.

JUST FOR FUN A and B

1. Pretend you are the parrot. Retell the story. Read your story to the class. Start with the sentence, *A man in Puerto Rico owned me.*

2. Pretend you are the man. Retell the story. Read your story to the class. Start with the sentence, *I had a wonderful parrot.*

Chapter 15

Nolbu and Hyungbu
The Story of Two Brothers
a folktale from Korea

BEFORE YOU READ A and B

1. Look at picture 1. Have you ever seen plants like these? What kind of plants do you think they are?

2. Do you know any stories in which a kind person helped an animal and then the animal helped the person?

3. In this story, the younger brother is honest, kind, and poor. The older brother is selfish and rich. Which brother do you think will be successful in the end? Why?

WHILE YOU READ

1. Read to the end of paragraph 5. What do you think Nolbu will do?

2. Read to the end of paragraph 6. What do you think will happen when Nolbu opens his gourd?

3. Read to the end of paragraph 7. What do you think Hyungbu will do when his older brother comes to him for help?

Nolbu and Hyungbu

The Story of Two Brothers

1   A long time ago, there were two brothers, Nolbu and Hyungbu. Nolbu, the older brother, was rich and greedy. Hyungbu, the younger brother, was the opposite. He was poor and generous.

2   Hyungbu's seven children were so hungry that they were going to die. Hyungbu decided to ask his brother Nolbu and his wife for some rice. But Nolbu's wife didn't want to give him any. She hit him in the face with the rice spoon. Hyungbu was so hungry that he took the little bit of rice on his face and ate it! Then he asked her to hit his face on the other side. This time, the sister-in-law hit him with a clean spoon.

3   On his way home, Hyungbu found a swallow with a broken leg. He took care of the bird. Then he let it fly away.

4   The next spring, the swallow brought a gourd seed to Hyungbu. Hyungbu planted it in the ground, and in the autumn he had many gourds.

5   When he cut open the gourds, pieces of gold fell out. After that, he became very rich and lived in a big house. His greedy brother came to him and asked, "How can you be so rich?" Hyungbu told him the truth.

6   After Nolbu left Hyungbu's house, he found a swallow. He broke the swallow's leg. Then he took care of it. When the bird was well again, he let it fly away. The next year the swallow brought him a gourd seed. He planted it in the spring, and in the fall he harvested it.

7   When Nolbu opened the gourd, dirty water came out. The water covered his house and his farm. Suddenly he became a poor man. He had nothing to eat and no place to sleep.

8   He went to Hyungbu's house and asked for help. Good Hyungbu gave him food to eat and a warm place to sleep.

9   Then Nolbu understood his mistakes. He decided to be a good person. The two families lived happily together for the rest of their lives.

COMPREHENSION

1 *Write* **T** *next to the sentences that are* **true***. Write* **F** *next to the sentences that are* **false***.*

1. _____ Nolbu broke a swallow's leg.

2. _____ Nolbu's wife hit Nolbu with a spoon.

3. _____ Nolbu's gourds were filled with dirty water.

4. _____ Hyungbu became rich.

5. _____ Hyungbu was a good person.

6. _____ Hyungbu helped Nolbu when Nolbu was poor.

7. _____ Nolbu helped Hyungbu when Hyungbu was poor.

8. _____ Hyungbu helped a swallow with a broken leg.

9. _____ In the spring, Hyungbu had many gourds.

2 *Number the sentences to show the correct story order.*

_____ Hyungbu asked his sister-in-law for rice.

_____ Nolbu broke the swallow's leg.

_____ Hyungbu's children were very hungry.

_____ Hyungbu opened a gourd, and gold fell out.

_____ Nolbu became a poor man.

_____ A swallow brought Hyungbu a gourd seed.

_____ Nolbu planted his gourd seed.

_____ Hyungbu gave his brother food and a place to sleep.

3 *Answer the following questions in pairs or small groups.*

1. What words at the end mean the same as "They lived happily ever after"?

2. What did Nolbu's wife do when Hyungbu asked her for food?

3. What did the swallow bring Hyungbu? Why did the swallow help him?

4. What was inside Hyungbu's gourd?

5. What was inside Nolbu's gourd?

6. Was Nolbu a nice person? How do you know?

7. Was Hyungbu a nice person? How do you know?

8. What kind of animal is a swallow? What word in paragraphs 3 helps you guess the answer?

VOCABULARY

1 Match the words in the first column with the words that mean the opposite in the second column.

1. _____ rich   **a.** older
2. _____ the autumn   **b.** the spring
3. _____ greedy   **c.** poor
4. _____ younger   **d.** harvested
5. _____ broke   **e.** fixed
6. _____ planted   **f.** a lie
7. _____ the truth   **g.** generous

2 Complete the sentences with words from the list.

swallow	greedy	generous
opposite	truth	sister-in-law

1. A person who always wants more money is _____ .
2. Maria heard a _____ singing in a tree.
3. It is important to always tell the _____ .
4. Hyungbu was kind, but his brother was the _____ .
5. She gives a lot of money to charity because she is _____ .
6. I was very happy when my brother and _____ got married.

GRAMMAR

Write the simple past tense form of these verbs.

Base	Past	Base	Past
1. seem	_____	7. let	_____
2. live	_____	8. break	_____
3. eat	_____	9. help	_____
4. find	_____	10. become	_____
5. plant	_____	11. take	_____
6. bring	_____	12. come	_____

WHILE YOU READ

1. Read to the end of paragraph 5. What do you think Nolbu will do?

2. Read to the end of paragraph 6. What do you think will happen when Nolbu opens his gourd?

3. Read to the end of paragraph 7. What do you think Hyungbu will do when his older brother comes to him for help?

Nolbu and Hyungbu

The Story of Two Brothers

1   Once there were two brothers. Although Nolbu, the older one, was rich and greedy, Hyungbu, the younger brother, was poor and generous.

2   One day, when Hyungbu's seven children were starving, he went to his brother to ask for rice to feed them. But when Hyungbu's sister-in-law saw him, she did not want to give him any rice. Instead she hit him on the cheek with the rice scoop. Hyungbu was so hungry that he ate the little bit of rice on his face. Then he turned the other cheek and told her to hit him again. This time she hit him with a clean scoop.

3   On his way home, Hyungbu found a swallow whose leg was broken. He took care of it until it was well, and then he let it fly away.

4   When spring came, the swallow brought Hyungbu a gourd seed to plant. In the fall, after he harvested the gourds, Hyungbu opened one of them. Gold coins poured out! Then he became a rich man.

5   Nolbu was jealous because his younger brother now had a big house with a beautiful garden. He wanted to know how Hyungbu became so rich. So Hyungbu told him exactly what had happened.

6   On the way home from Hyungbu's house, Nolbu found a swallow. He broke its leg and then cared for it. After it got better, he let it fly away. The following year, the swallow brought him a gourd seed. Nolbu did just what Hyungbu had done.

7   But in the autumn, when Nolbu opened his gourd, there was no gold. Instead, dirty water poured out of it. The water flooded his house and farm. Suddenly he was a poor man with no food and no roof over his head!

8   Nolbu didn't know what to do. He begged Hyungbu for help, and of course his kind brother said yes.

9   Then Nolbu understood his own faults. He made up his mind to be a better person. He, his brother, and their families lived together happily for the rest of their lives.

COMPREHENSION

1 *Answer the following questions in pairs or small groups.*

1. In paragraph 5 it says, *So Hyungbu told him exactly what had happened.* What did Hyungbu tell him about?

2. How was what Nolbu did different from what Hyungbu did?

3. In paragraph 7 it says, *Suddenly he was a poor man with no food and no roof over his head*. This means

   a. his house lost its roof.

   b. his house was destroyed.

   c. his roof was wet.

   d. his house never had a roof.

4. Why do you think Hyungbu received a gourd seed that would grow gold-filled gourds and Nolbu received a seed that grew dirty, water-filled gourds?

2 *Circle the words that describe each character.*

1. Which words describe Nolbu at the beginning of the story?

   generous   greedy   rich   poor   mean   selfish

2. Which words describe Hyungbu at the beginning of the story?

   hungry   poor   selfish   greedy   generous   kind

3. Which words describe Nolbu's wife at the beginning of the story?

   single   generous   considerate   impolite   mean   rich

4. Which words describe Hyungbu at the end of the story?

   hungry   poor   rich   kind   selfish   greedy

5. Which words describe Nolbu at the end of the story?

   poor   rich   sorry   angry   greedy   nice

VOCABULARY

1 Look back at the story. Find the synonyms for the underlined words.

1. Which word in paragraph 2 means <u>very, very hungry</u>?

   _____

2. Which word in paragraph 2 means <u>side of the face</u>?

   _____

3. Which word in paragraph 2 means <u>big spoon or ladle</u>?

   _____

4. Which word in paragraph 3 means <u>a kind of bird</u>?

   _____

5. Which word in paragraph 4 means <u>picked ripe fruits or vegetables</u>?

   _____

6. Which phrase in paragraph 5 means <u>what had taken place</u>?

   _____

7. Which phrase in paragraph 6 means <u>looked after, nursed, tended</u>?

   _____

8. Which phrase in paragraph 6 means <u>did the same thing as</u>?

   _____

9. Which word in paragraph 7 means the same as the word <u>fall</u> in paragraph 4?

   _____

10. Which phrase in paragraph 9 means <u>decided</u>?

    _____

2 *Match the words in the first column with their definitions in the second column.*

1. _____ greedy
2. _____ starving
3. _____ a scoop
4. _____ a gourd
5. _____ harvested
6. _____ jealous
7. _____ poured
8. _____ following
9. _____ flooded
10. _____ a roof
11. _____ begged
12. _____ made up one's mind

a. a kind of spoon
b. next
c. always wanting to have more things or money
d. very, very hungry
e. covered with water
f. flowed or spilled steadily
g. wanting what another person has
h. the top of a house
i. decided
j. a fruit with a hard shell
k. asked for very strongly
l. picked crops

DICTIONARY SKILLS

Use your dictionary to find the definition and part of speech for each underlined word as it is used in the sentence.

1. The <u>following</u> spring, the swallow brought him a gourd seed.

   definition _____

   part of speech _____

2. Please stop <u>following</u> me, or I will call the police.

   definition _____

   part of speech _____

3. The following <u>spring</u>, the swallow brought him a gourd seed.

   definition _____

   part of speech _____

4. The <u>spring</u> in my mattress is broken.

   definition _____

   part of speech _____

5. The following spring, the <u>swallow</u> brought him a gourd seed.

definition _____

part of speech _____

6. Because she had a sore throat, it hurt her to <u>swallow</u> hot food.

definition _____

part of speech _____

7. In the <u>fall</u>, he harvested the gourds.

definition _____

part of speech _____

8. Don't let the baby <u>fall</u> into the water.

definition _____

part of speech _____

GRAMMAR

Combine each pair of sentences using the word in parentheses.

1. Hyungbu found a swallow. Its leg was broken.

(whose) _____

2. Hyungbu harvested the gourds. He opened one.

(after) _____

3. Nolbu was jealous. His younger brother now had a big house.

(because) _____

4. His younger brother had a big house. It had a garden.

(with) _____

5. Nolbu opened his gourd. There was no gold in it.

(when) _____

6. Suddenly he was a poor man. He had no food and no roof over his head.

(with) _____

DISCUSSION AND WRITING

Discuss or write answers to these questions.

1. *Make up one's mind* means "to decide." Nolbu made up his mind to be a better person. Give an example of something you made up your mind to do. Were you successful? Then, give an example of something you made up your mind to do but didn't do.

2. If you were Hyungbu, would you help your brother Nolbu? Why or why not?

3. What kind of person was Hyungbu at the beginning of the story? What kind of person was Nolbu? How did they change? Why?

4. Is there another story in this book, or another story that you know, that talks about greed? Are the two stories alike in any way? How are they different?

JUST FOR FUN A and B

1. In small groups, write and act out a play based on this story. Use props to help you act out what happens.

2. In pairs, write a story on a different subject using at least five of the following words. Read your stories to the class.

generous	greedy	rich	considerate	selfish
mean	hungry	starving	kind	generous
married	single	poor	angry	sorry

Chapter 16

THE GOLDEN AX

a folktale from China

BEFORE YOU READ A and B

1. Look at the picture. Do you think the boy threw the ax, or do you think it fell? How can you tell?

2. If someone found something valuable that did not belong to you and asked you if it was yours, what would you do?

3. Like many stories about brothers and sisters, this story is about brothers who are very different from each other. Are you different from people in your family? How are you different? Why do you think brothers and sisters can be so different?

1. Discuss the saying "Honesty is the best policy." What does it mean? As you read the story, think about which brother follows that saying and which one does not.

2. Read to the end of paragraph 6. How do you think the story will end?

THE GOLDEN AX

1   A long time ago, two brothers lived in a small village. The younger brother was Li Gang, and the older brother was Li Ping.

2   Every morning, the brothers crossed over a small river to go to work. One morning when Li Gang crossed the bridge, his ax fell into the river. He sat down and cried.

3   Suddenly he saw an old man in front of him. The old man asked him why he was crying. Li Gang said, "I dropped my ax into the water and now I cannot work." Then the old man went away.

4   Soon he returned with a silver ax. Li Gang looked at it and said, "That is not my ax." Then the man brought another ax. It was made of gold. But Li Gang said it was not his ax.

5   Finally the old man showed him an iron ax. Li Gang said, "That is the ax I lost." The old man said, "You are an honest boy. I will give you your ax and the golden ax, too."

6   When Li Gang got home, he told his brother about the man and the axes. But his brother didn't believe it. So the next morning, Li Ping went to the river and dropped his ax from the bridge. Then he started to cry loudly.

7   The old man came. Li Ping told him that he had dropped his ax. Li Ping asked for help.

8   When the old man brought the silver ax to him, Li Ping said that it was his. Then the old man showed him the golden ax. He said that the golden ax was also his.

9   But the old man was unhappy. He said, "You are not an honest boy. You cannot keep the silver ax or the golden ax. And I will not return your iron ax." Then the old man went away and no one ever saw him again.

COMPREHENSION

1 *Write **T** next to the sentences that are **true**. Write **F** next to the sentences that are **false**.*

1. _____ Li Gang was the older brother.

2. _____ Li Ping was an honest boy.

3. _____ Li Ping dropped a silver ax.

4. _____ Li Ping dropped his ax down a mountain.

5. _____ At the end of the story, Li Ping didn't have any axes.

6. _____ Li Ping dropped his ax by mistake.

7. _____ Li Gang dropped his ax by mistake.

8. _____ The old man gave Li Gang a golden ax.

2 *Number the sentences to show the correct story order.*

_____ Li Gang dropped his ax.

_____ Li Ping dropped his ax.

_____ Li Gang saw an old man in front of him.

_____ Li Ping told the old man the silver ax was his.

_____ The man gave Li Gang a golden ax.

3 *Answer the following questions in pairs or small groups.*

1. Why did the old man show Li Ping a golden ax?

2. Why did the old man give Li Gang a golden ax?

3. Why did Li Gang need an ax?

4. Where did the ax fall?

5. Why did the old man say that Li Ping was not an honest boy?

6. Who was the honest boy?

VOCABULARY

Match the words in the first column with their definitions in the second column.

1. _____ a village
2. _____ crossed
3. _____ a bridge
4. _____ an ax
5. _____ suddenly
6. _____ dropped
7. _____ finally
8. ___ honest

a. quickly and unexpectedly
b. a small town
c. went from one side to the other
d. in the end
e. a tool used for cutting wood
f. let fall
g. truthful
h. a structure built over something, such as a river, so people can go over it

GRAMMAR

Look back at the story. Find the sentence in the paragraph shown in parentheses. Then, tell who or what the underlined word refers to.

1. . . . the <u>brothers</u> crossed over a small river . . . (paragraph 2)

   brothers _____

2. <u>He</u> sat down and cried. (paragraph 2)

   he _____

3. Li Gang looked at <u>it</u> and said, "<u>That</u> is not my ax." (paragraph 4)

   it _____ that _____

4. But <u>his</u> brother didn't believe <u>it</u>. (paragraph 6)

   his _____ it _____

5. . . . and no one ever saw <u>him</u> again. (paragraph 9)

   him _____

1. Discuss the saying "Honesty is the best policy." What does it mean? As you read the story, think about which brother follows that saying and which one does not.

2. Read to the end of paragraph 6. How do you think the story will end?

THE GOLDEN AX

1   A long time ago, two brothers lived together in a small village. The younger brother was called Li Gang, and the older brother was called Li Ping.

2   Every morning on their way to work, the brothers had to cross a bridge over a small river. One morning as Li Gang was crossing the bridge, he dropped his ax into the water by accident. He sat down and started to cry because he could not work without his ax.

3   Suddenly an old man appeared in front of him and asked why he was crying. After Li Gang explained what had happened, the old man disappeared.

4   When he returned, he was carrying a silver ax. Li Gang looked at it and said that it was not his. Then the old man brought another ax that was made of gold. But Li Gang said that one wasn't his either.

5   Finally the old man brought the old iron ax. Li Gang said, "Yes, that's it. That's the ax I lost." The old man told him that because he was an honest boy, he could have not only his own ax but also the golden ax.

6   When Li Gang got home, he told his brother what happened, but his brother did not believe the story. So the next morning, Li Ping went to the bridge and dropped his ax into the water on purpose. Then he began to weep loudly.

7   Soon the old man came. Li Ping explained what had happened and asked the old man for his help.

8   When the old man brought him the silver ax, Li Ping said that it was his, and when the old man brought the golden ax, Li Ping said that it was his also. "You are dishonest. You cannot have either of these axes, and I will not give back your iron ax," the old man said. Then he disappeared, and no one ever saw him again.

COMPREHENSION

Answer the following questions in pairs or small groups.

1. Which brother dropped his ax by accident? Which one dropped it on purpose?

2. Which brother was dishonest?

3. Why didn't the old man give Li Ping his ax?

4. *The old man told him that because he was an honest boy, he could have not only his own ax but also the golden ax.* This means

   a. he could not have his own ax or the golden ax.

   b. he could not have the golden ax.

   c. he could have only his ax.

   d. he could have both his ax and the golden ax.

VOCABULARY

1 *Match the words in the first column with the words or phrases that mean the opposite in the second column.*

1. _____ younger   **a.** dishonest

2. _____ dropped   **b.** left

3. _____ by accident   **c.** disappeared

4. _____ appeared   **d.** on purpose

5. _____ returned   **e.** to laugh

6. _____ honest   **f.** older

7. _____ to weep   **g.** softly

8. _____ loudly   **h.** picked up

2 *Circle the word or phrase in each row that is different from the others.*

1. laugh   cry   weep   sob
2. dishonest   trustworthy   truthful   honest
3. accidentally unintentionally on purpose   by accident
4. disappeared came   left   went away
5. village   hamlet   small town   city

Complete the sentences with words from the list.

| ax | bridge | explained | finally | village |

1. I _____ the problem to my friend.

2. The people lived in a small _____ , not a big city.

3. He used an _____ to cut down the tree.

4. We had to cross the _____ to get over the river.

5. We waited and waited, and our friend _____ arrived.

DICTIONARY SKILLS

Use your dictionary to find the definition and part of speech for each underlined word as it is used in the sentence.

1. The priest wore a <u>cross</u> around his neck.

   definition _____

   part of speech _____

2. The child was not allowed to <u>cross</u> the street alone.

   definition _____

   part of speech _____

3. Maria was tired and <u>cross</u> this morning.

   definition _____

   part of speech _____

4. John lost two teeth in the car accident, so the dentist gave him a <u>bridge</u>.

   definition _____

   part of speech _____

5. How can we <u>bridge</u> our differences and make peace?

   definition _____

   part of speech _____

6. I prefer to take the <u>bridge</u> instead of the tunnel when I have to cross the river.

   definition _____

   part of speech _____

7. When I get nervous, I sometimes <u>drop</u> things.

definition _____

part of speech _____

8. Ivan had to <u>drop</u> two classes this semester.

definition _____

part of speech _____

9. The ball game was canceled when the first <u>drop</u> of rain came.

definition _____

part of speech _____

10. The ax was made of <u>iron</u>.

definition _____

part of speech _____

11. Mark decided to surprise his wife and <u>iron</u> the clothes.

definition _____

part of speech _____

GRAMMAR

1 *Read each of the following sentences in indirect speech. Then, rewrite them in direct speech. Look back at page 9 if you need help. The first one is done for you.*

1. Li Gang looked at the ax and said that it was not his.

_____ Li Gang looked at the ax and said, "That is not mine." _____

2. The old man told him that because he was an honest boy, he could have not only his ax but also the golden ax.

_____

3. When the old man showed him the golden ax, Li Ping said that it was his also.

_____

2 *Rewrite the following sentences in indirect speech.*

1. Li Gang said to the old man, "That's the ax I lost."

_____

2. The old man said to Li Ping, "You are dishonest"

_____

3 Look back at the story. Find the sentence in the paragraph shown in parentheses. Then, tell who or what the underlined words refer to.

1. . . . Li Gang explained <u>what had happened</u> . . . (paragraph 3)

   What had happened?

   _____

2. . . . Li Gang looked at <u>it</u> and said that <u>it</u> was not his. (paragraph 4).

   What wasn't his? _____

3. But Li Gang said <u>that one</u> wasn't his either. (paragraph 4)

   What does *that one* refer to? _____

DISCUSSION AND WRITING A and B

Discuss or write answers to these questions.

1. Many stories have a moral, or lesson that they teach. This story shows that "Honesty is the best policy." Do you know any stories from your country that teach the same lesson?

2. What other stories in this book teach the same lesson?

JUST FOR FUN A and B

Find the following words in the puzzle. The words can be written across, up and down, forward, backward, or on an angle.

| either | believe | brother | gold | truth | iron | honest | silver |

```
g   b   r   o   t   h   e   r   s   h
o   i   e   e   r   i   o   n   d   r
m   i   v   t   s   e   n   o   h   t
s   p   e   i   g   e   l   r   s   k
n   i   i   o   d   i   n   i   o   t
h   a   l   h   r   t   r   u   t   h
o   d   e   v   i   h   h   e   i   o
s   t   b   s   e   e   g   l   d   n
v   l   v   t   i   r   d   t   o   i
h   k   o   r   h   e   u   f   r   s
```

Chapter 17

The Lion and the Hyena

a folktale from Africa

BEFORE YOU READ A and B

1. Look at the pictures. How many animals can you name?

2. What are some good ways to solve disagreements among friends?

3. Do you know someone who always wants to be in charge? What would you do if you and that person disagreed?

WHILE YOU READ

1. The lion is often called "the king of the jungle" or the "king of the beasts." As you read the story, decide whether you think the hyena or the lion is right. Why do you think most of the animals said the lion was right?

2. Stop at the end of paragraph 4. What do you think will happen next? Who do you think will get the baby cow?

■ ■ ■

The Lion and the Hyena

1   A long time ago, the lion was the king of the animals. He and the hyena were friends. They often went out to look for food together.

2   One day, they found a cow and a bull. The lion said to the hyena, "You can have the cow. I want the bull because it is powerful like me." The hyena was afraid of the lion, so he said yes.

3   The lion was very busy being king, so the hyena took care of the cow and the bull. One day the hyena said to the lion, "My cow will soon have a baby." When the baby cow was born, the lion went to look at it. "This isn't your cow's baby; it is my bull's baby!" said the lion to the hyena. Then the two friends disagreed.

4   They called all the old and wise animals to decide who owned the baby cow. All the animals came except the ape. They all said that the baby cow belonged to the lion. But as they were leaving, the ape finally arrived. "I was very busy," he said to the lion.

5   The lion shouted, "I'm king of the animals, but I'm here! Why were you too busy to come?" "I was sewing the earth and the sky together," the ape explained. Then the lion asked, "How is it possible to sew the earth and sky together?" "First tell me," the ape answered, "how is it possible for a bull to have a baby?"

COMPREHENSION

1 *Write* **T** *next to the sentences that are* **true***. Write* **F** *next to the sentences that are* **false***.*

1. _____ The hyena wanted to give the bull to the lion.

2. _____ The hyena took care of both the bull and the cow.

3. _____ The ape sewed the sky and earth together.

4. _____ The animals said the baby cow belonged to the lion.

5. _____ The bull gave birth to a baby.

6. _____ The lion was strong.

7. _____ The lion was king of the animals.

8. _____ The lion and the hyena were friends.

9. _____ The cow gave birth to a baby.

10. _____ The ape thought that the hyena should keep the baby cow.

2 *Number these sentences to show the correct story order.*

_____ The lion and the hyena found a bull and a cow.

_____ The ape explained why he was late.

_____ All the wise animals met to decide who owned the baby cow.

_____ The lion said he wanted the bull because it was strong.

_____ A baby cow was born.

3 *Answer the following questions in pairs or small groups.*

1. Why did the lion want the bull?

2. Why did the hyena let the lion have the bull?

3. How did the lion and hyena decide who owned the baby cow?

4. Why did the ape say he was late?

5. In this story:

    a. Which animal was wise?

    b. Which one took care of his animals?

    c. Which one was a "bully"?

    d. Which animals were strong?

    e. Which animal had a baby?

VOCABULARY

Match the words in the first column with their definitions in the second column.

1. _____ a hyena
2. _____ a bull
3. _____ powerful
4. _____ disagreed
5. _____ wise
6. _____ belonged to
7. _____ arrived
8. _____ possible
9. _____ to sew

a. was owned by
b. able to be done
c. had a different opinion from someone
d. strong
e. a male cow
f. having good sense; intelligent
g. to join together with a needle and thread
h. came
i. a wild animal that is like a dog

GRAMMAR

1 *Complete the sentences with the correct word forms.*

| disagree | disagrees | disagreed |
| disagreeable | disagreement | |

1. Sofia and Luis always _____ about which movie to see.
2. Lee is a _____ person.
3. The parents _____ about what to name the baby, so they asked the grandparents to decide.
4. Joe always _____ with the teacher about his homework.
5. They had a _____ about the class project.

Write three sentences using words from the list above.

_____

_____

_____

Look back at the story. Find the sentence in the paragraph shown in parentheses. Then, tell who or what the underlined words refer to.

1. "I want the bull because it is powerful like me." (paragraph 2)

   I _____ it _____ me _____

2. "This isn't your cow's baby; it is my bull's baby!" (paragraph 3)

   this _____ your _____ it _____

3. Then the two friends disagreed. (paragraph 3)

   two friends _____

4. But as they were leaving, the ape finally arrived. (paragraph 4)

   they _____

B WHILE YOU READ

1. The lion is often called "the king of the jungle" or "the king of the beasts." As you read the story, decide whether you think the hyena or the lion is right. Why do you think most of the animals said the lion was right?

2. Stop at the end of paragraph 4. What do you think will happen next? Who do you think will get the baby cow?

■ ■ ■

The Lion and the Hyena

1   Long ago, the lion, who was called the king of the beasts, and the hyena were good friends. Often they went together to search for food.

2   One day, while the two friends were out, they found a cow and a bull. The lion told the hyena to take the cow. The lion added, "I will take the bull, which is powerful like me." The hyena agreed because he was afraid of the lion.

3   After a while, the cow gave birth to a calf. The two friends fought over the calf; each claimed that it belonged to him.

4   Finally they called all the wise animals to judge who was right. When all the animals but the ape had gathered together, they decided that the lion owned the new calf. But just as they were getting ready to leave, the ape came. He apologized for being late. "I was very busy," he told the lion.

5   "Why were you so busy?" shouted the lion. The ape explained that he had been sewing the earth and sky together. When the lion asked how that was possible, the ape replied, "First tell me, how is it possible for a bull to have a baby?"

COMPREHENSION

An **inference** is something you can guess to be true based on information that you already know. Answer the following questions by making inferences about the story.

1. Do you think the ape was really sewing the sky and earth together?
2. Why do you think the ape said that?
3. Why did the other animals want to give the calf to the lion?
4. Did the ape want to give the calf to the lion or the hyena?
5. Who was the calf's father?

VOCABULARY

Match the words in the first column with their definitions in the second column.

1. _____ beasts   **a.** came together
2. _____ to search   **b.** said very loudly
3. _____ a calf   **c.** wild animals
4. _____ claimed   **d.** said, "I'm sorry."
5. _____ to judge   **e.** stitching
6. _____ gathered   **f.** to look for
7. _____ apologized   **g.** a baby cow
8. _____ shouted   **h.** to decide
9. _____ sewing   **i.** said something was true

DICTIONARY SKILLS

Use your dictionary to find the definition and part of speech for each underlined word as it is used in the sentence.

1. Nikki has her <u>own</u> car.

    definition _____

    part of speech _____

2. I <u>own</u> two dogs.

    definition _____

    part of speech _____

3. The man almost drowned because he got a <u>stitch</u> in his side while he was swimming.

definition _____

part of speech _____

4. Did the ape really <u>stitch</u> the sky and earth together?

definition _____

part of speech _____

5. Tom sat in the dark because the <u>power</u> was out in his neighborhood.

definition _____

part of speech _____

6. The president of the company has a lot of <u>power</u>.

definition _____

part of speech _____

GRAMMAR

1 *Look back at the story. Find the sentence in the paragraph shown in parentheses. Then, tell who or what the underlined words or phrases refer to.*

1. . . . <u>the king of the beasts</u>, and the hyena were good friends. (paragraph 1)

the king of the beasts _____

2. <u>The two friends</u> fought over the calf; <u>each</u> claimed that <u>it</u> belonged to him. (paragraph 3)

the two friends _____

each _____

it _____

3. But just as <u>they</u> were getting ready to leave, the ape came. (paragraph 4)

they _____

2 *Combine each pair of sentences using the words or instructions in parentheses.*

1. The lion was called the king of beasts. The lion and the hyena were friends.

(who) _____

2. I will take the bull. It is powerful like me.

(which) _____

3. They were getting ready to leave. The ape came.

   (just as) _____

4. All the animals gathered. They decided the calf belonged to the lion.

   (when) _____

5. The hyena agreed. He was afraid of the lion.

   (because) _____

6. They went together. They searched for food.

   (Use the infinitive.) _____

3 When a story is *chronological*, it is told in time order. Chronological stories use transition words to show the connection between one idea and the next. The following transition words show time relationships in the story.

long ago	one day	after a while	finally

Look to see where and how each of these words or phrases was used in the story. On a separate piece of paper, write a paragraph using at least three of these transition words.

DISCUSSION AND WRITING A and B

Discuss or write answers to these questions.

1. Who do you think got the calf? Why?

2. Why do you think most of the animals agreed with the lion?

3. Who did the ape think should get the calf? How do you know?

4. In what ways was the lion a "bully"?

5. Were you ever in a situation in which you thought that someone who had power over you was wrong? Did you agree with that person because you were afraid, or did you speak up?

JUST FOR FUN A and B

Hold a pretend trial to decide who should get the calf. Decide who will be the judge, lion, hyena, lion's lawyer, and hyena's lawyer. The rest of the class will be the jury.

Chapter 18

Why Female Mosquitoes Bite

a folktale from Vietnam

BEFORE YOU READ A and B

1. What is a mosquito? What does the title tell you about mosquitoes? What else do you know about them?

2. Like "The Ant and the Cicada," this story is told to explain something in nature. Do you know other stories that try to explain facts about nature?

3. Look at picture 1. The man looks very sad. Read the story to find out what happened.

A WHILE YOU READ

1. Read to the end of paragraph 5. What do you think will happen next?

2. Which is more important to you, love or money? As you read, see which choice the woman makes.

Why Female Mosquitoes Bite

1   Many years ago in Vietnam, a poor fisherman lived with his beautiful wife. The fisherman was happy, but his wife was not. She wanted to be rich.

2   One day when the fisherman was working, his wife became sick and died. The fisherman came home and found his wife dead. He sat near her and prayed.

3   While he was praying, he heard a voice. The voice told him how to bring his wife back to life. The voice said, "Cut your finger and let three drops of blood fall on your wife." The man did what he was told. And when the third drop of blood fell on his wife, she came back to life. The fisherman was very happy to have his wife back.

4   One day soon after that, the wife went to the beach to wait for her husband to come back from fishing. While she was waiting, she met a rich man with a big boat. The rich man told the woman, "You are very beautiful. Come with me on my big boat. I can make you very wealthy." The woman wanted to be rich, so she went with him.

5   When her husband came back, he saw two other fishermen. They told him that his wife had left with the rich man. The husband went to find his wife. When he found her, he was very angry. He asked her to come back home, but she would not. Then he told her that he wanted back his three drops of blood.

6   He cut her hand with a knife, and three drops of blood fell. Then the woman changed. She became very small and grew wings. She flew around her husband's head angrily saying, "Give me back the three drops of blood!"

7   To this day, female mosquitoes still fly around trying to get back those three drops of blood!

COMPREHENSION

1 *Write* **T** *next to the sentences that are* **true**. *Write* **F** *next to the sentences that are* **false**.

1. _____ The wife was happy with her husband.

2. _____ The husband was a fisherman.

3. _____ The husband loved his wife.

4. _____ The fisherman brought his wife back to life.

5. _____ The wife went with the rich man.

6. _____ The fisherman got his three drops of blood back.

7. _____ The wife turned into a mosquito.

8. _____ The wife was very beautiful.

9. _____ The man gave his wife four drops of blood.

2 *Number these sentences to show the correct story order.*

_____ The wife went on the rich man's boat.

_____ The wife became sick and died.

_____ The wife became small and grew wings.

_____ The fisherman asked his wife to come back to him.

_____ The fisherman gave his wife three drops of blood.

_____ The fisherman went to find his wife.

_____ The fisherman cut his wife's hand.

_____ The fisherman prayed for his dead wife.

3 *Answer the following questions in pairs or small groups.*

1. Why wasn't the wife happy with her husband?

2. How did the husband learn how to bring his wife back to life?

3. How did the husband bring his wife back to life?

4. Where did the wife meet the rich man?

5. What happened to the wife when the husband took his blood back?

6. According to this story, why do female mosquitoes bite?

VOCABULARY

Match the words in the first column with their definitions in the second column.

1. _____ beautiful   a. glad
2. _____ happy   b. to drop down
3. _____ rich   c. to return
4. _____ to fall   d. wealthy
5. _____ to come back   e. mad
6. _____ a boat   f. a small ship
7. _____ angry   g. very pretty

GRAMMAR

1 Complete the sentences with the correct word forms.

| dies | died | dead | death | dying |

1. Her grandmother became sick and _____ last year.
2. The police found a _____ body this morning.
3. His _____ was a surprise because he was so young.
4. Every day a child _____ from hunger somewhere in the world.
5. As he was _____ , the thief told the police where he had hidden the money.

2 Look back at the story. Find the sentence in the paragraph shown in parentheses. Then, tell who or what the underlined words refer to.

1. The man did <u>what he was told</u>. (paragraph 3). What did he do?

   _____

2. One day <u>soon after that</u>, the wife went to the beach . . . (paragraph 4). Soon after what? _____

3. . . . but <u>she would not</u>. (paragraph 5). Who is *she*? What wouldn't she do?

   _____

PRONUNCIATION AND SPELLING

1 **Kn** *is pronounced* **n** *in* **knife**. *What are three other words in which* **kn** *is pronounced* **n**?

_____ _____ _____

2 *The plural of* **mosquito** *is* **mosquitoes**. *Many words that end in* -**o** *add* -**es** *for the plural. What are three other words that end in* -**o** *and add* -**es** *to make the plural? Use your dictionary if you need help.*

_____ _____ _____

3 Usually, words add -**s** to form plurals, but some plurals are irregular.

    Example: fisherman   fishermen

Write the plural for these words. Use your dictionary if you need help.

Singular	Plural
1. wife	_____
2. knife	_____
3. life	_____
4. man	_____
5. woman	_____
6. child	_____
7. person	_____
8. foot	_____

For some irregular verbs, there are no rules for making the plural form. For others, there are. Look at the words in the list above. Can you make a rule to explain the plurals of words ending in -**fe** *and* -**man**?

-fe _____

-man _____

WHILE YOU READ

1. Read to the end of paragraph 5. What do you think will happen next?

2. Which is more important to you, love or money? As you read, see which choice the woman makes.

Why Female Mosquitoes Bite

1   Many years ago in Vietnam, there lived a poor fisherman and his beautiful wife. The fisherman was happy, but his wife was not. She wanted to be wealthy.

2   One day while the husband was out fishing, the wife became ill and died. When he came home and found her dead, the fisherman was very sad. He sat near her and prayed.

3   While he was praying, he heard a voice telling him how to bring her back to life. The voice told him to cut his finger and let three drops of blood fall on his wife. The fisherman followed these instructions. As the third drop of blood fell on his wife, she came back to life. How happy he was to have his wife back!

4   One day shortly after that, the wife went down to the beach to wait for her husband to return from fishing. While she was waiting, she met a rich merchant with a large boat. The man told her that she was very beautiful and asked her to come with him on his big boat. He promised to make her rich, so she went with him.

5   When her husband returned, the other fishermen told him that his wife had gone off with the rich man. The husband went to find his wife, and when he did, he was very angry. He asked her to come home, but she refused. Then he demanded that she give him back his three drops of blood.

6   With a knife, he cut her hand. When the third drop of blood fell, the woman changed. She became very tiny. She flew around her husband's head buzzing angrily and demanding that he give her back the three drops of blood.

7   And to this day, female mosquitoes still fly around trying to get back their three drops blood!

COMPREHENSION

1 *Answer the following questions in pairs or small groups.*

1. What did the man do when he found his wife dead? How did he know what to do?

2. Why did the wife go with the merchant?

3. Why do you think the wife refused to go home with her husband?

4. What did the man do when his wife refused to return with him?

2 *Circle the words that describe each character in the story. Use your dictionary if you need help.*

1. Which words describe the fisherman in paragraphs 1, 2, and 3?

   happy   praying   rich   poor   angry   greedy   vengeful   loving

2. Which words describe the fisherman in paragraphs 4, 5, 6, and 7?

   happy   praying   rich   poor   angry   greedy   vengeful   loving

3. Which words describe the wife in paragraphs 1, 2, and 3?

   unhappy   beautiful   dead   greedy   poor   selfish   vengeful   winged

4. Which words describe the wife in paragraphs 4, 5, 6, and 7?

   unhappy   beautiful   dead   greedy   poor   selfish   vengeful   winged

VOCABULARY

1 *Match the words in the first column with their definitions in the second column.*

1. _____ mosquitoes   **a.** a small amount of liquid

2. _____ to bite   **b.** a person who buys and sells goods

3. _____ wealthy   **c.** asked for strongly

4. _____ ill   **d.** small insects that bite

5. _____ followed instructions   **e.** to put teeth or a stinger into something

6. _____ a drop   **f.** very small

7. _____ shortly   **g.** said no

8. _____ a merchant   **h.** did as one was told

9. _____ refused   **i.** making a low noise (like the sound of a bee)

10. _____ demanded   **j.** sick

11. _____ tiny   **k.** rich

12. _____ buzzing   **l.** very soon

2 *Circle the word in each row that means the opposite of the first word.*

1. **husband**   spouse   mate   wife   brother

2. **poor**   penniless   rich   happy   money

3. **happy**   glad   smile   sad   tired

4. **tiny**   small   little   unusual   big

5. **dead**   tired   sick   alive   asleep

6. **refused**   asked   answered   agreed   denied

7. **ill**   sick   angry   dead   healthy

8. **beautiful**   ugly   sick   young   lovely

9. **return**   circle   leave   come back   turn around

10. **female**   woman   husband   wife   male

3 *Complete the sentences with words from the list.*

buzzes	demanded	followed	gone off	tiny
merchant	mosquito	refused	wealthy	

1. Because the _____ was very _____ , he owned a big boat.

2. Although the _____ is a very _____ insect, it is very annoying because it _____ around people's heads.

3. When the poor people _____ food, the mean king _____ to get it for them.

4. When the fisherman learned that his wife had _____ with a rich man, he _____ her.

DICTIONARY SKILLS

Use your dictionary to find the definition and part of speech of each underlined word as it is used in the sentence.

1. The wife said, "I <u>refuse</u> to come home."

   definition _____

   part of speech _____

2. Please don't leave your <u>refuse</u> in front of my house.

   definition _____

   part of speech _____

3. The saleswoman said, "I'll be with you <u>shortly</u>."

   definition _____

   part of speech _____

4. The customer replied <u>shortly</u>, "I want service now!"

   definition _____

   part of speech _____

5. There was a <u>buzz</u> in the room when the famous actress entered.

   definition _____

   part of speech _____

6. I don't like when bees <u>buzz</u> around my head.

   definition _____

   part of speech _____

7. Does Mr. Lee always <u>buzz</u> his secretary when he wants her to come to his office?

   definition _____

   part of speech _____

GRAMMAR

1 Sentences that make a very strong point are called *exclamations*. Their word order is sometimes different from the word order used in regular statements. *How* is followed by an adjective, and *what* is followed by a noun phrase. An exclamation point (!) ends the sentence.

Statement:	He was happy to have his wife back.
Exclamation:	How happy he was to have his wife back!
Statement:	This is a great surprise.
Exclamation:	What a great surprise this is!

Change these exclamations to statements.

1. How good it is to see you!

_____

2. What a good boy you are!

_____

Change these statements to exclamations.

3. That is a terrific idea.

_____

4. You must be so happy about the new baby.

_____

2 *Look back at the story. Find the sentence in the paragraph shown in parentheses. Then, write who or what the underlined words refer to.*

1. . . . but his wife <u>was not</u>. (paragraph 1). What was she not?

_____

2. The fisherman followed <u>these instructions</u>. (paragraph 3).
What instructions did he follow? _____

3. . . . <u>when he did</u>, he was very angry. (paragraph 5) Who was *he*?
When he did what? _____

4. . . . but <u>she refused</u>. (paragraph 5) Who is *she*? What did she refuse
to do? _____

DISCUSSION AND WRITING

Discuss or write answers to these questions.

1. What is said in the story that makes it clear that the fisherman loved his wife?

2. Was the husband right to take back the three drops of blood?

3. What would you have done in the wife's place when the merchant asked her to come with him? What would you have done in the husband's place when you found that your wife had gone off with the merchant?

4. How are "The Ant and the Cicada," "The Mountain God and the River God," and "Why Female Mosquitoes Bite" alike? What natural event is explained by each story?

JUST FOR FUN A and B

1. Hold a court hearing to decide if the fisherman should give his wife back the three drops of blood. Use vocabulary that you learned in "A Thief's Story." Select people to be the fisherman, the wife, the rich merchant, and the witnesses (other fishermen) who saw the wife leave. Pick a judge, a lawyer for the wife, and a lawyer for the fisherman. The rest of the class is the jury.

2. Working in pairs, make a list of words using the letters in the word *mosquitoes*.

    Examples: it

    some

    quite

Chapter 19

THE SMARTEST ANIMAL

BEFORE YOU READ A and B

1. Look at picture 1. The buffalo is helping the man on the farm. What are some other animals that help on a farm? How do they help?

2. What animal do you think is the smartest? Why?

3. What do you think is better, intelligence or strength? Why?

WHILE YOU READ

1. Read to the end of paragraph 3. What do you think will happen next?

2. Read to the end of paragraph 4. Why do you think the man really tied the tiger to the tree?

THE SMARTEST ANIMAL

1   Once there was a farmer in Laos. Every morning and every evening he plowed his field with his buffalo.

2   One day a tiger saw the farmer and his buffalo working. The tiger was surprised to see a big animal listening to a small animal. He wanted to know more about the buffalo and the man.

3   After the man went home, the tiger spoke to the buffalo. "You are so big and strong. Why do you do everything that the man tells you?" The buffalo answered, "Oh, the man is very intelligent." The tiger asked, "Can you tell me how intelligent he is?" "No, I can't tell you," said the buffalo, "but you can ask him."

4   So the next day the tiger said to the man, "Can I see your intelligence?" But the man answered, "It's at home." "Can you go and get it?" asked the tiger. "Yes," said the man, "but I'm afraid you will kill my buffalo when I am gone. Can I tie you to a tree?"

5   After the man tied the tiger to the tree, he didn't go home to get his intelligence. He took his plow and hit the tiger. Then he said, "Now you *know* about my intelligence even if you haven't *seen* it."

COMPREHENSION

1 *Write* **T** *next to the sentences that are* **true**. *Write* **F** *next to the sentences that are* **false**.

1. _____ The man really left his intelligence at home.

2. _____ The man went home to get his intelligence.

3. _____ The man tied up the tiger.

4. _____ The farmer plowed his field every morning and every evening.

5. _____ The farmer was intelligent.

6. _____ The buffalo was stronger than the man.

2 *Number the sentences to show the correct story order.*

_____ The man hit the tiger with the plow.

_____ The buffalo said that the man was very intelligent.

_____ The man said that he had left his intelligence at home.

_____ The tiger saw the man plow his field with the buffalo.

_____ The tiger asked the buffalo a question.

VOCABULARY

Circle the word in each row that is different from the others. Use your dictionary if you need help.

1. intelligent   foolish   smart   wise

2. afraid   frightened   scared   brave

3. answered   replied   said   asked

4. listen to   obey   heed   disobey

GRAMMAR

Complete the sentences with the correct word forms.

intelligence	intelligent	intelligently

1. The man in the story was very _____ .

2. He acted very _____ when he tied up the tiger.

3. The buffalo knew about the man's _____ .

surprise	surprised	surprising	surprisingly

4. The test was _____ easy.

5. My mother promised me a _____ for my birthday.

6. The boy was happy and _____ when his mother gave him a puppy.

7. My cat is constantly _____ me with his intelligence.

The Smartest Animal | **163**

WHILE YOU READ

1. Read to the end of paragraph 3. What do you think will happen next?

2. Read to the end of paragraph 4. Why do you think the man really tied the tiger to the tree?

■ ■ ■

THE SMARTEST ANIMAL

1   There was once a Laotian farmer who plowed his field every morning and every evening with his buffalo.

2   One day a tiger saw the farmer and the buffalo working together. The tiger was surprised to see such a big animal obeying such a small one. He was curious about the buffalo and the man.

3   After the man went home, the tiger went up to the buffalo and said, "I want to ask you something. You are so big and strong. Why do you obey the little man?" The buffalo answered, "Because the man is so intelligent." Then the tiger asked, "Can you tell me how intelligent he is?" "No, I can't tell you," said the buffalo, "but why don't you ask him?"

4   The next day the tiger asked the man to show him his intelligence. But the man answered that it was at home. The tiger asked the man to go home and get it. The man said that he would, but he would have to tie up the tiger so he couldn't hurt the buffalo. The tiger agreed.

5   But after he tied up the tiger, the man didn't go home to get his intelligence. Instead, he took the plow and hit the tiger with it. Then he said, "Now you *know* about my intelligence, even if you haven't *seen* it."

COMPREHENSION

1 *Answer the following questions in pairs or small groups.*

1. *The tiger was surprised to see such a big animal obeying such a small one.* What was the big animal? What was the small animal?

2. Why did the buffalo listen to the man?

3. What work did the buffalo do on the farm?

4. Why did the man tie up the tiger?

5. Why did the man hit the tiger?

6. According to this story, what is the smartest animal?

2 *Write the words under the animal they describe. Some words might describe more than one animal. Use your dictionary if you need help.*

hardworking	intelligent	strong	big	smart
obedient	curious	small	sly	foolish

Tiger   **Man**   **Buffalo**

_____   _____   _____

_____   _____   _____

_____   _____   _____

_____   _____   _____

VOCABULARY

Complete the sentences with words from the list.

buffalo	curious	intelligence	obey	plowed

1. The _____ , like the ox and the horse, is an animal that farmers use to do work on a farm.

2. He _____ the field before he planted the seeds.

3. Children do not always _____ their parents.

4. Sometimes being too _____ can get you in trouble.

5. _____ means the "ability to learn and understand."

DICTIONARY SKILLS

Use your dictionary to find the definition and part of speech for each underlined word as it is used in the sentence.

1. He gets up early every morning to <u>plow</u> his field.

   definition _____

   part of speech _____

2. The man used a <u>plow</u> when he worked in his field.

   definition _____

   part of speech _____

3. The businessman wore a jacket and <u>tie</u> to work.

   definition _____

   part of speech _____

4. I like to <u>tie</u> holiday packages with red ribbon.

   definition _____

   part of speech _____

5. The baseball game was <u>tied</u> in the ninth inning.

   definition _____

   part of speech _____

6. The farmer planted crops in his <u>field</u>.

   definition _____

   part of speech _____

7. The football <u>field</u> was wet after the rain.

   definition _____

   part of speech _____

8. The baseball player tried to <u>field</u> the ball.

   definition _____

   part of speech _____

GRAMMAR

1 *Look back at the story. Find the sentence in the paragraph shown in parentheses. Then, write who or what the underlined words refer to.*

1. The tiger was surprised to see such a <u>big animal</u> obeying such a <u>small one</u>. (paragraph 2)

   big animal_____ small one _____

2. . . . "but why don't <u>you</u> ask <u>him</u>?" (paragraph 3)

   you _____ him _____

3. The tiger asked the man to go home and get <u>it</u>. (paragraph 4)

   it _____

4. The man said that <u>he</u> <u>would</u> . . . (paragraph 4) Who is *he*? What would he do?

   he _____ would _____

5. The tiger <u>agreed</u>. (paragraph 4) What did he agree to?

   agreed _____

2 *Rewrite the following sentences in direct speech. Look back at page 9 if you need help.*

1. The tiger asked the man to show him his intelligence.

   _____

2. But the man answered that it was at home.

   _____

3. The tiger asked the man to go home and get it.

   _____

4. The man said that he would, but he would have to tie up the tiger so he couldn't hurt the buffalo.

   _____

5. The tiger agreed.

   _____

3 *Rewrite the following sentences in indirect speech.*

1. The tiger said to the buffalo, "I want to ask you something."

    _____

2. The tiger asked the buffalo, "Why do you obey the little man?"

    _____

3. The buffalo answered, "Because the man is so intelligent."

    _____

DISCUSSION AND WRITING

Discuss or write the answers to these questions.

1. Which animals do you think are the smartest animals? Why? Which animals do you think are the strongest animals? Why?

2. Do you think the man was smart or cruel in his treatment of the tiger? Explain.

JUST FOR FUN

1. Act out this story in groups of three. Use a few simple props to help explain what is going on.

2. Pretend you are the tiger. Retell the story. Start with the sentence, *One day I saw a farmer and a buffalo working together.*

3. Pretend you are the man. Retell the story. Start with the sentence, *I plowed my field every morning and every evening with my buffalo.*

Chapter 20

Bouki Rents a Horse

a folktale from Haiti

BEFORE YOU READ   A and B

1. Bouki is a common character in Haitian folktales. He is easily fooled. Do you know any other stories with a character who is foolish or easily fooled?

2. Malice is also a common character in Haitian folktales. He is sometimes mean but always clever. Do you know any other stories about a character who is clever?

3. Look at picture 1. Does the man look happy or sad? Why do you think he feels that way?

WHILE YOU READ

1. Read to the end of paragraph 4. How do you think Malice will help Bouki?

2. As you are reading, decide whether Bouki should have trusted Malice.

■ ■ ■

Bouki Rents a Horse

1   Bouki worked hard in his garden all year. Finally it was time to dig up his vegetables and take them to the market. He took his hoe and dug up a big pile of yams. He looked at the big pile and thought, "How can I take all of these to the market? Maybe I can borrow my friend Moussa's donkey."

2   He asked his friend Moussa for the donkey, but Moussa said, "I'm sorry, my donkey ran away. I've been looking for him all day." "Oh, no," said Bouki, "I must take my yams to the market tomorrow. What can I do?" Moussa said, "Why don't you ask Toussaint? Maybe you can borrow his horse." Bouki replied, "You know Toussaint won't lend anything to anyone! He might *rent* me the horse, but he'll charge me more than the price of the yams!"

3   But finally Bouki went to Toussaint's house. "Honor," Bouki said. "Respect," replied Toussaint, for that is how people greet one another in Haiti. "Please, Mr. Toussaint," Bouki said. "I need your horse to take my yams to the market tomorrow." Toussaint answered, "My horse is too good to take yams to market. But for you, friend Bouki, I will rent him for fifteen coins." "Fifteen!" cried Bouki. "That is as much as I'll get for my yams. I have only five." Toussaint quickly took Bouki's five coins and said, "You can bring me the other ten when you come to get the horse tomorrow morning."

4   Early the next morning when Bouki got up to go to the market, Moussa was at his front door with his donkey. Moussa explained, "He came home last night. You can borrow him to take your yams to the market." "Oh," said Bouki sadly. "I rented Toussaint's horse. I already gave him five coins, and you know he won't give me my money back." Just then, Malice came along and heard Bouki's problem. "I can get your money back and even get a little extra for my trouble. I'll go with you to see Toussaint."

5   Bouki and Malice went to Toussaint's house. "We are here for the horse," said Malice. "Give me the ten coins and you can have the horse,"

replied Toussaint. "Just a minute," said Malice. "I have to see if the horse is big enough." He pulled a tape measure out of his pocket and began to measure the horse.

6   Malice said, "You can sit in the middle, Bouki. We need about 18 inches for you. I'll sit behind you. We need about 15 inches for me. My wife can sit behind me. She will take about 18 inches. Madame Bouki can sit in front of you. She will need about 20 inches."

7   "Wait," shouted Toussaint. You can't put *four* people on my horse!" "Oh, we aren't putting four people on the horse," said Malice, as he measured the horse's neck. "The children will fit here, but it will be crowded."

8   "No," shouted Toussaint. You can't put that many people on my horse. You will kill him! You can't have the horse." "Yes, we can. Bouki rented him from you," yelled Malice. "You already took his money." "Here are his five coins. I'm renting him back from you," Toussaint exclaimed.

9   Malice replied, "Five coins? You were going to charge us fifteen and you want to rent him back from us for five? Do you think we are stupid?" "But Bouki gave me only five coins," complained Toussaint. Suddenly, Bouki asked, "Can we fit Grandmother on the horse? She wants to go to the market, too." "Here," shouted Toussaint. "Take your fifteen coins and leave my horse alone!"

10   Toussaint took his horse and walked away. Bouki and Malice just laughed and laughed. Then Bouki stopped laughing and said seriously, "I don't think Grandmother would fit on the horse."

COMPREHENSION

1 Write **T** *next to the sentences that are* **true**. *Write* **F** *next to the sentences that are* **false**.

1. _____ Moussa has a horse.

2. _____ Bouki wants to rent Moussa's donkey.

3. _____ Toussaint wanted to rent his horse for five coins.

4. _____ Bouki gave Toussaint five coins.

5. _____ Moussa's donkey ran away.

6. _____ Malice wanted to put four people on the horse.

7. _____ Toussaint measured the horse.

8. _____ Moussa's donkey came home.

9. _____ Toussaint gave Malice fifteen coins for his own horse.

10. _____ Bouki believed that Malice was going to put many people on the horse.

2 **Number the sentences to show the correct story order.**

_____ Bouki gave Toussaint five coins.

_____ Bouki dug up his yams.

_____ Toussaint said, "You can't put four people on my horse!"

_____ Malice measured the horse.

_____ Toussaint gave Malice fifteen coins.

_____ Bouki asked to borrow Moussa's donkey.

_____ Bouki said, "I don't think Grandmother would fit on the horse."

_____ Malice said, "I can get your money back."

3 **Answer the following questions in pairs or small groups.**

1. What crop did Bouki grow in his garden?

2. Why didn't Moussa lend Bouki the donkey when Bouki asked for it?

3. Where does this story take place?

4. Where did Bouki want to take his yams?

5. What are the words people use to greet each other in Haiti?

6. How much did Toussaint want to charge to rent his horse?

7. How did Malice get Toussaint to change his mind about renting the horse?

8. Why did Bouki change his mind about renting Tossaint's horse?

VOCABULARY

Match the words in the first column with the words that mean the opposite in the second column.

1. _____ lend   **a.** borrow

2. _____ respect   **b.** behind

3. _____ night   **c.** dishonor

4. _____ in front of   **d.** whispered

5. _____ yelled   **e.** smart

6. _____ stupid   **f.** morning

GRAMMAR

Look back at the story. Find the sentence in the paragraph shown in parentheses.
Then, write who or what the underlined words refer to.

1. "I've been looking for <u>him</u> all day." (paragraph 2)

   I _____ him _____

2. "But for <u>you</u>, friend Bouki, <u>I</u> will rent <u>him</u> for fifteen coins." (paragraph 3)

   you _____ I _____ him _____

3. "<u>I</u> already gave <u>him</u> five coins, and <u>you</u> know he won't give me my money back."
   (paragraph 4)

   I _____ him _____ you _____

B WHILE YOU READ

1. Read to the end of paragraph 4. How do you think Malice will help Bouki?
2. As you are reading, decide whether Bouki should have trusted Malice.

■ ■ ■

Bouki Rents a Horse

1   Bouki tended his garden carefully all year. Finally it was time to harvest his crops; he took his hoe and dug up a pile of yams. He looked at the big stack of yams and wondered how he could get them to the market. He thought that his generous friend, Moussa, might lend him a donkey.

2   But when Bouki asked Moussa to let him borrow the donkey, Moussa said sadly, "My donkey ran away yesterday. I've been looking for him all day." Bouki was upset and said, "Oh, no. I must take my yams to the market tomorrow. What can I do?" Moussa suggested that Bouki borrow Toussaint's horse. "Old stingy Toussaint never lent anything to anyone in his life," said Bouki. "He might *rent* me the horse, but he'll probably charge me more than the price of the yams!"

3   Finally Bouki went to Toussaint's house. "Honor," Bouki said. "Respect," Toussaint replied, for that is how people greet one another in Haiti. Bouki asked Toussaint for his horse to take the crops to market the next day. As Bouki had predicted, Toussaint offered to rent the horse for fifteen coins. Bouki replied that he wouldn't get much more than that for

his yams, and besides, he had only five coins with him. Toussaint quickly grabbed Bouki's five coins and told him to bring the other ten the next day when he came for the horse.

4   Early the next morning when Bouki got up to go to the market, Moussa was waiting for him. His donkey had returned, and he offered to lend it to Bouki. But Bouki sadly explained that he had already given Toussaint a deposit of five coins to rent the horse. Both men knew that greedy old Toussaint would not return the deposit. Just then, Malice came along, and Bouki explained the situation to him. Malice replied, "I can get Toussaint to return your deposit and I'll even get a little extra money from him for my trouble. I'll go with you to see Toussaint; just let me do all the talking."

5   Bouki and Malice arrived at Toussaint's house. Malice said he wanted to see the horse that Bouki had rented. Toussaint asked for his ten coins, but Malice said that he had to see if the horse was big enough first. He pulled a tape measure from his pocket and began to measure the horse.

6   Malice said to Bouki, "You can sit in the middle, and we need 18 inches for you. I can sit behind you and I need about 15 inches. Now I can put my wife behind me, and she will need about 18 inches, and of course lovely Madame Bouki can sit in front of you. She will need at least 20 inches."

7   "Wait!" shrieked Toussaint. "You can't put four people on my horse!" "Oh, we aren't putting *four* people on your horse," replied Malice as he measured the horse's neck. "The children will fit here, but it will be crowded."

8   "No!" screamed Toussaint. "You can't put that many people on my horse. You'll kill him. You can't have my horse." "Yes, we can. Bouki rented him from you," yelled Malice. "You already took his deposit." Toussaint replied, "Here are the five coins. I'm renting him back from you."

9   Malice said, "We are both smart businessmen. You were going to rent the horse to us for fifteen coins. Certainly you don't expect us to rent him back to you for less." "B-B-But," answered Toussaint, "Bouki gave me a deposit of only five coins." Suddenly, Bouki spoke up. "Can we fit Grandmother on the horse somewhere? She wants to go to the market, too." "Here," shouted Toussaint, putting fifteen coins into Malice's hand. "Take the money and get away from my horse!"

10   Toussaint took his horse and marched away. Bouki and Malice laughed so hard that they fell down. Then they just rolled on the ground in laughter. Suddenly, Bouki stopped laughing and said seriously to Malice, "I don't think we could have fit Grandmother on the horse anyway."

COMPREHENSION

Answer the following questions in pairs or small groups.

1. Look at paragraph 6. Who is bigger, Malice or Bouki? Who is smaller, Madame Malice or Madame Bouki? How do you know?

2. Does Malice really intend to put a lot of people on Toussaint's horse? How do you know?

3. Does Toussaint believe that Malice wants to put a lot of people on the horse? How do you know?

4. Did Bouki believe that Malice wanted to put a lot of people on the horse? How do you know?

VOCABULARY

 Circle the word in each row that has a different meaning from the others. Use your dictionary if you need help.

1. yell   scream   shriek   want

2. pile   stack   crops   heap

3. reply   answer   ask   respond

2 *Write the words under the person they describe. You do not have to fill in all of the blank lines. Use your dictionary if you need help.*

stingy	generous	kind	hardworking	nice
cheap	greedy	foolish	confused	selfish
friendly	happy	smart	tricky	clever

Toussaint	Bouki	Malice	Moussa
_____	_____	_____	_____
_____	_____	_____	_____
_____	_____	_____	_____
_____	_____	_____	_____
_____	_____	_____	_____

DICTIONARY SKILLS

Use your dictionary to find the definition and part of speech for each underlined word as it is used in the sentence.

1. Malice began to <u>measure</u> the horse.

   definition _____

   part of speech _____

2. Malice took an unusual <u>measure</u> to get the deposit back for Bouki.

   definition _____

   part of speech _____

3. Waltz music has three beats to the <u>measure</u>.

   definition _____

   part of speech _____

4. Bouki decided to harvest his <u>crops</u>.

   definition _____

   part of speech _____

5. Gina <u>crops</u> her hair every summer.

   definition _____

   part of speech _____

6. Bouki gave Toussaint a <u>deposit</u> of five coins.

   definition _____

   part of speech _____

7. If I don't <u>deposit</u> money in my bank account, I won't be able to pay my bills.

   definition _____

   part of speech _____

GRAMMAR

Look back at the story. Find the sentence in the paragraph shown in parentheses. Then, write who or what the underlined words refer to.

1. Bouki replied that he wouldn't get much more than <u>that</u> for his yams . . . . (paragraph 3)

   that _____

2. Toussaint quickly grabbed Bouki's five coins and told him to bring the <u>other ten</u> the next day. (paragraph 3)

   other ten _____

3. <u>He</u> pulled a tape measure from his pocket and began to measure the horse. (paragraph 5)

   he _____

4. Then <u>they</u> just rolled on the ground in laughter. (paragraph 10)

   they _____

DISCUSSION AND WRITING

1. Bouki is a character in many Haitian tales. Like Juan Bobo, Bouki is often foolish or misunderstands things. What did he misunderstand in this story?

2. Malice is also a character in many Haitian tales. Sometimes he is mean, but he is always tricky or clever. What did he do in this story that was tricky or clever?

3. Do you think Malice was wrong to trick Toussaint? Why or why not?

JUST FOR FUN A and B

1. Divide the class into three groups. If you are in the first group, pretend you are Bouki and retell the story. If you are in the second group, pretend you are Toussaint and retell the story. If you are in the third group, pretend you are Malice and retell the story. Each group will read or present its version of the story to the class.

2. Act out the story in groups. Use a few simple props to help explain what is going on.

Glossary

A

accident (n) something bad that happens and is not planned

accuse (v) to say someone did something wrong; to blame

admire (v) to approve of; to respect; to like

advice (n) a suggestion about what someone should do about a problem or situation

agree (v) to have the same opinion as someone else

alarm (n) something that warns of danger; (v) to give a warning to someone

alike (adj) almost the same; similar; (adv) in the same or a similar way

amazed (adj) very surprised

angry (adj) unhappy or upset with someone or something; annoyed; irritated

ant (n) a small insect that lives in groups, doesn't fly, and works very hard

anthill (n) a small pile of earth that ants build to live in

ape (n) a large animal that is like a monkey

appear (v) to begin to be seen; to become visible

appreciate (v) to be grateful for; to be thankful for

argument (n) a disagreement

arrest (v) to be caught by the police for doing something wrong and be brought to a police station

arrive (v) to come; to get to a place

arrow (n) a thin, pointed stick that is shot from a bow and is used as a weapon (see *bow and arrow*)

ashamed (adj) how people feel when they do something wrong; guilty

ask for the hand of (v) to ask to marry

astonished (adj) very surprised

attack (v) to start a fight; to try to hurt someone or something, usually with violence

awake (v) to stop sleeping; to wake up

awoke (v) the past tense of *awake* (see *awake*)

ax (n) a tool for cutting wood

B

bag (n) a container, made of cloth, leather, or paper

banquet (n) a formal meal for many people

bargain (n) an agreement to do or give something in return for something else

bark (n) the sound a dog makes; (v) to make the sound of a dog

beach (n) an area covered with sand or stones next to an ocean, sea, lake, or river

beast (n) a wild animal

beautiful (adj) very pretty

beg (v) to ask for something very strongly

belong to (v) to be owned by

below (adv) in a lower place; under

besides (adv) in addition to; also

billy goat (n) a male goat (see *goat*)

blanket (n) a warm cover for a bed

borrow (v) to take something from someone, and then give it back later

both (pron) two people or things together

bow (n) a long, thin, curved piece of wood with string at both ends used to shoot arrows (see *bow and arrow*)

bow and arrow (n) a kind of weapon

bowl (n) a deep, rounded dish that holds food or liquids

branch (n) a part of a tree that has leaves, fruit, or smaller branches growing from it

breakfast (n) the meal you eat in the morning

bridge (n) something that connects two sides of a river or a road so people or cars can go from one side to the other side

bring (v) to carry or take

broom (n) a large brush with a long handle that is used to sweep the floor

brought (v) the past tense of *bring* (see *bring*)

buffalo (n) a large animal that is like a cow, with a large head and thick hair

bull (n) a male cow

butt (v) to hit or push with the head

buzz (v) to make the noise that bees, mosquitoes, and other insects make

C

character (n) a person in a book, play, or movie

charge (v) to ask for money for something you are selling

chase away (v) to make something or someone go away

chat (v) to talk in a friendly, informal way

check (v) to see if something is right; to make sure

chili pepper (n) a very hot, spicy fruit

chilly (adj) cold enough to be uncomfortable; cool

cicada (n) a kind of insect that makes a loud, high noise

claim (v) to say something is true

clever (adj) smart; able to learn things quickly

climb (v) to move up, down, or across something using hands and feet

coin (n) a piece of money made of metal that is usually small, flat, and round

complete (adj) finished; (v) to finish

confused (adj) not able to understand; not sure

contest (n) a test of who is best at something

continue (v) to keep happening or to keep doing something without stopping

convince (v) to make someone believe something; to persuade

corn (n) a tall plant with yellow seeds that are cooked and used for food. In some countries, corn is called *maize*.

countryside (n) the land outside cities and towns

court (n) a room or building where a judge, lawyers, and other people make decisions about the law

cover (v) to put something on or over something else

cramp (n) a quick, sharp pain that makes it difficult to move

crawl (v) to move slowly on hands and knees, or with the body close to the ground

crime (n) an action that is against the law

crop (n) a plant such as grain, fruits, or vegetables that is grown to eat and use

crowd (n) a large group of people

crowded (adj) too full of people or things

culture (n) the beliefs, customs, and way of life of a group of people

custom (n) a tradition; a special way that a person or group does something

D

damp (adj) a little wet

dare (v) to be brave enough to do something

daughter (n) a mother or father's female child

dead (adj) not alive; not living

decide (v) to make a choice about something

delicious (adj) having a very good taste

demand (v) to ask strongly for something

deposit (n) money given for something to be bought or rented later

dig (v) to break up and move earth or make a hole in the ground

disagree (v) to have a different opinion from someone else

disappear (v) to go out of sight suddenly; to become impossible to see

distance (n) the amount of space separating two things

donkey (n) a gray or brown animal that is like a horse and is used for farm work

drown (v) to die from being under water too long

dug (v) the past tense of *dig* (see *dig*)

E

eagerly (adv) with great interest

emergency (n) an unexpected and dangerous situation that needs immediate action

empty (adj) having nothing inside

end (n) the last part or farthest point of something

enough (adj) as much as is needed

enter (v) to go or come into a place

except (prep) not including; other than; apart from

exchange (v) to give something to someone in return for something else

exclaim (v) to say strongly and suddenly

exhausted (adj) very tired

expect (v) to plan to have

F

famous (adj) well-known

farmer (n) a person who grows crops or raises animals

fault (n) responsibility for a mistake

fellow (n) a man

field (n) a piece of land used for a certain purpose, such as to keep animals or grow crops

file (n) a steel tool with a rough side used to make things smooth

finally (adv) in the end

fine (adj) very nice or of very good quality

finish (v) to come to the end of doing something; to complete

finish line (n) the place where a race ends

fisherman (n) someone who catches fish for sport or as a job

fit (v) to be the right size or shape for

flow (v) to move in a slow, steady way, especially liquid

folktales (n) stories told by people in a certain culture or ethnic group

fool (n) a stupid person

foolish (adj) silly; not reasonable or wise

forgive (v) to tell someone you are not angry about something that person did

fox (n) a small wild animal that is like a dog, with dark red fur, a pointed face, and a thick tail

frighten (v) to make someone or something feel afraid

frightened (adj) feeling afraid, scared

funny (adj) making someone laugh; amusing

furious (adj) very angry

G

generous (adj) ready to give money or help

gentle (adj) kind; calm; soft

get even (v) to hurt someone the same way that he or she hurt you; to make things even

goat (n) a four-legged farm animal that is like a sheep and has horns on its head

gourd (n) a large fruit with a hard shell that grows on a vine

grab (v) to take hold of someone or something quickly

grandchild (n) the child of a person's son or daughter

grant (v) to give something to someone

grateful (adj) feeling or showing thanks to someone

greedy (adj) always wanting to get too much of something; wanting to get more than what is fair

greet (v) to say hello; to welcome when meeting

ground (n) the surface of the earth; soil

H

hang (v) to tie something at the top so the top can't move but the bottom can, such as on a clothes hanger, on a hook, or on a rope

hare (n) an animal that is like a large rabbit, with longer ears and longer back legs

harvest (v) to pick crops

herd (n) a group of animals of the same kind

highlands (n) an area with a lot of mountains

hoe (n) a garden tool used for digging

honest (adj) truthful and sincere; not lying

honor (n) respect

horns (n) two hard pointed parts that grow on the top of the heads of some animals, such as goats, sheep, and cattle

hunter (n) a person who chases or kills animals usually for food

hurt (v) to cause or give pain

hyena (n) a wild animal that is like a dog and makes a sound like a laugh

I

identical (adj) exactly the same

identify (v) to say or show who someone is or what something is

industrious (adj) hardworking

insect (n) a very small animal that doesn't have bones and has six legs and a body with three parts

instructions (n) information or directions that tell how to do something

intelligent (adj) very smart

invite (v) to ask someone to go somewhere or do something

iron (n) a common, heavy metal used to make steel

J

jail (n) a place where criminals go for punishment; prison

jealous (adj) feeling unhappy or angry because you want what another person has

joke (n) a story or action that is funny

judge (n) a person that controls a court and makes decisions about the law; (v) to decide

K

kick (v) to hit with the feet

kid (v) to joke; to tease; to try to be funny

kind (n) type of; (adj) friendly, generous, good

L

lay down (v) the past tense of *lie down* (see *lie down*)

lazy (adj) not liking work or physical activity

leave alone (v) to stop worrying, bothering, or annoying someone

lend (v) to let someone use something for a certain amount of time

lie down (v) to put one's body in a flat position

lift (v) to raise; to pick up

lion (n) a wild animal that is like a cat but very large and with yellow-brown fur

loose (adj) not tied or held tightly; not attached to anything

lucky (adj) having good things happen

M

madame (n) French for *Mrs.*

malice (n) the desire to hurt others

manage (v) to be able to do something difficult

march (v) to walk with regular, even steps like a soldier

market (n) a place where people buy and sell goods or food

mean (adj) not nice; cruel

measure (v) to find the size, length, or amount of something

Midas touch (n) in stories: the ability to turn things into gold; in business: the ability to succeed or to become rich

miss (v) to feel sad because someone is not near

mistake (n) something that was done the wrong way; an error

mixed up (adj) confused

moral (n) a lesson from a story about what is right and wrong

mosquito (n) a small flying insect that bites and takes blood from people and animals

N

native town (n) the place where a person was born

needle (n) a small, thin, pointed piece of metal that has a hole in one end for thread and is used for sewing

neighbor (n) a person who lives near another person

noise (n) loud or unpleasant sounds

notice (v) to see, hear, or smell something

nowadays (adv) in present times

O

obey (v) to do what you are told to do

offer (v) to give something to someone; to say one will do something

ought to (v) should

outsmart (v) to trick

oversleep (v) to sleep too long or too late

overtake (v) to go ahead of someone or something

overwork (v) to work too hard

P

pack (n) a group of wild animals that live and hunt together

pain (n) a feeling of hurt in a particular part of the body

pair (n) two things of the same kind that are used together

parrot (n) a brightly-colored tropical bird that can make sounds like a person

patch (n) a small piece of cloth or material; a small piece of land, especially a small garden

patient (adj) having the ability to work or wait calmly without getting angry or complaining

pattern (n) a design made of shapes, colors, or lines

piece (n) a small part of something bigger; bits

pile (n) a group of things put on top of each other

pitcher (n) a tall container for holding and pouring liquids

plain (adj) very simple; not beautiful

please (v) to make someone feel happy

plow (n) a farming tool used to break up and turn over earth

point (v) to show something by holding out a finger toward it

pole (n) a long stick

polish (v) to rub something to make it shiny or clean

possess (v) to have or to own something

powerful (adj) very strong

pray (v), to ask for help or give thanks to God or a god

predict (v) to say what will happen in the future

prepare (v) to get ready; to make plans for something that is going to happen

price (n) the amount of money that something costs

princess (n) the daughter of a king or queen, or the wife of a prince

prison (n) a place where criminals go for punishment; jail

probably (adv) likely to happen or be true

problem (n) something that is difficult; trouble

promise (v) to tell someone that you will do something

promptly (adv) on time; quickly

pull loose (v) to get free

pumpkin (n) a large, round, orange-colored fruit that grows on a vine on the ground

Q

quick (adj) fast

quilt (n) a warm, thick cover for a bed made by sewing different layers or pieces of material together

R

rabbit (n) a small animal that has long ears and hops quickly

race (n) a competition to see who is the fastest; (v) to run quickly

ram (n) a male sheep

reach (v) to arrive at; to get to

realize (v) to understand and believe something that you did not know before

refuse (v) to say "no" to something

rent (n) the money paid to live in a place or to use something that belongs to someone else; (v) to pay money to live in a place or to use something that belongs to someone else

repeat (v) to say or do something again

reply (n) an answer; (v) to give an answer to someone

reputation (n) what people think about someone or something

request (n) something asked for in a nice, polite way; (v) to ask for something in a polite way

rescue (v) to save someone or something from danger; to set free

respect (n) honor, polite treatment; (v) to admire, to treat politely

response (n) an answer

result (n) something that happens because of something else that happened first

return (v) to go back or come back to a place; to give something back

rich (adj) wealthy; having a lot of money

ripe (adj) fully grown; mature

rise (v) to go up; to move to a higher place

rivalry (n) a competition between people who want to do better than each other

roadside (n) the area along a road or street

roll (v) to move by turning over and over

rope (n) a strong, thick string, often used for tying

S

safe (adj) not in danger of being harmed or destroyed

safety (n) being safe; being out of danger

satisfied (adj) pleased, happy; having enough

scare (v) to make someone feel afraid or nervous

scared (adj) afraid or nervous

scissors (n) a tool used for cutting paper, cloth, or other material

scoop (n) a deep, round spoon

scream (v) to yell; to cry angrily and loudly

señor (n) Spanish for *Mr.* or man

seriously (adv) sincerely; not in a joking way

several (quantifier, adj) some; more than a few, but not many

sew (v) to join pieces of cloth together with a needle and thread; to stitch

sharp (adj) having a thin edge that can cut things easily; having a fine point

sharpen (v) to make a point or an edge

sheep (n) a four-legged farm animal that gives us wool

shepherd (n) someone who takes care of sheep

shine (v) to give off light; to look bright

shiver (v) to shake from cold or fear

shocked (adj) very surprised

short (adj) not long; not tall

shortly (adv) very soon

shovel (n) a tool with a long handle and a wide end used for digging or moving earth or snow

shriek (n) a scream; (v) to scream; to cry angrily and loudly

silly (adj) foolish; not serious

smash (v) to break into many pieces

smashed (adj) broken into pieces, usually with violence or force

starting line (n) the place where a race begins

starving (adj) very, very hungry; suffering from hunger

steadily (adv) at an even speed; with firm, balanced movements

steal (v) to take something that belongs to someone else

stick (n) a long, thin piece of wood

stingy (adj) not liking to give or share; cheap

stitch (v) to join pieces of cloth together using a needle and thread; to sew

stomp (v) to walk heavily; to step hard on the ground

stork (n) a tall, white bird with a long beak, neck, and legs

stranger (n) a person who is not known, unfamiliar

strip (n) a long, narrow piece of cloth or paper

stupid (adj) not smart; not having good sense

succeed (v) to do well

suggest (v) to say or write an idea

sure enough (adv) certainly; happening the way something was meant to happen

swallow (n) a small bird with pointed wings

sweep (v) to use a broom to clean a floor

swim (v) to move through water by using your arms and legs

T

tape measure (n) a long narrow strip of cloth or metal marked with inches or centimeters and used to measure things

thick (adj) not thin; measuring a large distance from side to side

thought (n) an idea

thought (v) past tense of *think*

thread (n) a long, thin string used to sew

tiger (n) a wild animal like a cat, but very large and with yellow fur with black lines

tiny (adj) very small

tomato (n) a soft, round, red fruit that is often eaten as a vegetable

tortoise (n) an animal that is like a turtle, but that lives on land (see *turtle*)

town (n) a small city

townspeople (n) the people who live in a town

trick (v) to fool someone; to deceive

trouble (n) a difficult or dangerous situation

turtle (n) an animal that has a hard shell, moves slowly, and lives mostly in the water

U

unique (adj) the only one of its kind; unusual

unpopular (adj) not liked by many people

upset (adj) worried; feeling unhappy about something

V

vegetable (n) a plant that people eat, such as corn, lettuce, or potatoes

village (n) a very small town or group of houses in a country area

villagers (n) the people who live in a village

W

water buffalo (n) a large animal like a cow that has horns and is often used to work on farms

wealthy (adj) rich; having a lot of money

wing (n) the part of an insect or bird that allows the insect or bird to fly

wise (adj) having good sense; able to understand what happens and decide the right action

wolf (n) a wild animal that is like a dog and hunts other animals

wonder (v) to want to know what is true; (n) something surprising or very good

wonderful (adj) very good

wooden (adj) made from wood (the material from a tree)

world (n) the earth

worried (adj) thinking about a problem; concerned; anxious

Y

yam (n) another name for *sweet potato*

yell (v) to shout or say something loudly